THE FIRST NINETY DAYS

THE FIRST NINETY DAYS

MOVING FROM CO-WORKER TO MANAGER

Published 2026 by Gildan Media LLC
aka G&D Media
www.GandDmedia.com

THE FIRST NINETY DAYS. Copyright © 2026 by Pryor Learning, LLC. All rights reserved.

No part of this book may be used, reproduced or transmitted in any manner whatsoever, by any means (electronic, photocopying, recording, or otherwise), without the prior written permission of the author, except in the case of brief quotations embodied in critical articles and reviews. No liability is assumed with respect to the use of the information contained within. Although every precaution has been taken, the author and publisher assume no liability for errors or omissions. Neither is any liability assumed for damages resulting from the use of the information contained herein.

Front cover design by David Rheinhardt of Pyrographx

Interior design by Meghan Day Healey of Story Horse, LLC

Library of Congress Cataloging-in-Publication Data is available upon request

ISBN: 978-1-7225-0735-0

10 9 8 7 6 5 4 3 2 1

CONTENTS

FOREWORD 7

ONE
Management Styles and General Management
— 11 —

TWO
How to Avoid the Most Common Mistakes
— 39 —

THREE
Building Teamwork
— 71 —

FOUR
Unlocking Your Executive Presence
— 99 —

FIVE
Optimal Communication Styles
— 123 —

SIX
Conquering Procrastination
— 159 —

SEVEN
Strategic Problem-Solving
— 185 —

EIGHT
Developing a Growth Mindset
— 211 —

AFTERWORD 235

FOREWORD

Pryor Learning has been at the forefront of corporate training, shaping the skills and careers of millions. Founded more than fifty years ago, when Fred Pryor pioneered the "one-day seminar," Pryor Learning has become one of the nation's leading training providers, offering efficient, affordable, and accessible career education for business professionals. Our diverse offerings cater to a wide array of individuals and organizations alike, from small and midsized businesses to governments, nonprofits, and Fortune 500 companies.

Offering thousands of seminars annually, Pryor Learning is synonymous with practical, hands-on training that delivers results. As the workforce continues to evolve, so do we—embracing new technologies and expanding our reach. Today we offer a vast array of training options including in-person, live virtual, and on-demand formats, all designed to meet the diverse needs of a constantly changing workplace.

This book, along with the series it belongs to, represents the next step in our mission to empower professionals with the essential skills they need to excel. In response to the growing popularity of e-books and audiobooks, we aim to reach a new generation of learners, equipping them with the tools and knowledge to thrive in their careers. Our goal remains simple: to uphold Fred Pryor's legacy by making high-quality business training accessible to all, regardless of where they are in their career journey.

Join us in a tradition of learning that spans more than fifty years—a tradition that has empowered millions to achieve their professional goals. We invite you to explore the wealth of knowledge contained within these pages, knowing that you are part of something greater—a community dedicated to continual growth and improvement.

This volume in our learning series focuses on one key moment of career growth: the transition from staff member to manager. Although the basic skills required remain the same, others will be required, not only to cope with the added responsibilities but to ensure continued personal growth and satisfaction.

This volume explores the central issues that confront the fledgling manager: everything from understanding your own management style to dealing with employees who are personal friends or who have tried for the same job.

The following chapters will explore such areas as management style; common management mistakes; building teamwork; enhancing executive presence; improving communication styles; conquering procrastination; strategic problem-solving; and developing a growth mindset.

Although these topics are to a certain extent crucial at every career level, they are particularly important for the new manager to master—ideally in the first ninety days on the job. This book provides insights, tips, and systems for coping with the most common management problems, bringing the best out in a team, and inspiring yourself and those you manage.

ONE

Management Styles and General Management

When you move from being a staff member to supervisor, it's useful to start by taking a look at the different types of management styles and seeing where you fit in with your personality and skill set. You should also consider what you *want* to be. These two can be in line or out of alignment with each other. It's all about being consistent. You may want to be one type of management style, yet your personality and skills make you better suited to another type. As you look at these different management styles, be brutally honest with yourself about which style really fits you.

Management Styles

The first style is *autocratic*. An autocratic style means that the manager makes decisions unilaterally and generally without much regard for his or her subordinates. As a result, decisions will reflect the opinions and personality of the manager. In other words, the manager is right and everybody else is wrong. These managers do what they think is best. They don't involve their subordinates in evaluating decisions.

Next is the *consultative*. This is a more paternalistic style. Decisions take into account the best interest of the employees as well as of the business. Although communication is generally downward, feedback to management is encouraged to maintain morale, although it is not necessarily taken into account. This kind of manager listens to what subordinates have to say in order to make them feel as if they're involved, but does not take into account what they say or allow it to influence their decision. Consultative managers do what they think is best for the employees, the department, and the company—and that's it.

The *democratic* style involves employees to a much greater degree. The majority rules. Employees take part in the decision-making, and everything is agreed upon by the majority. Communication is extensive in both directions: up and down.

This style can be particularly useful in conflicts or decisions that require a range of specialized skills. Say you are in a department that has a number of specialties or a very technical environment, where a number of different skill sets all need to contribute their input to come up with a true solution to a problem. Here a democratic management style could be most useful.

Another option: you can combine the consultative and democratic management styles. In this situation, you're listening to what everybody has to say and taking all suggestions and ideas into account, but in the end, you're processing them all yourself and making what you think is the best decision.

> **Management Styles**
> 1. Autocratic
> 2. Consultative
> 3. Democratic
> 4. Fair
> 5. Management by walking around

With a *fair* leadership style, the leader's role is more that of a mentor and a stimulator. It's a very hands-off approach. The staff manages their own jobs. This kind of manager is essentially saying, "I'm going to teach you, I'm going to mentor you, I'm going to work with you, and I'm going to try to inspire you to do your job, but I'm going to leave you alone to go ahead and do your job."

Then there is *management by walking around*. This classic technique is used by managers who are proactive listeners. They're out there, talking to employees and gathering information. This is more of an informal scenario. Rather than having staff meetings where everybody reports in (although you can do that as well), you walk around, chat with your employees, and discuss what's going on. You're using your interpersonal skills and listening skills to understand what's going on. This is quite an effective way.

It's very rare that any manager is a pure embodiment of any of these styles. More often, some combination is involved. With the consultative style, the manager is the one that makes the final decision. In some respects, this is standard, because in the end, the managers are responsible for the decisions that are made. But you can also incorporate the democratic style: it's not so much that the majority rules, but you're listening to all of your staff. Combining the consultative and democratic styles with management by walking around can create a nice mix. You're the one that needs to make the final decision, because you're responsible for it, but, using the democratic style, you realize that everybody has a valued opinion. Management by walking around coordinates well with the democratic style, because here the manager is going out and getting the staff's opinions.

Key Requirements for Management

We've already touched upon one important tip about transitioning into a supervisory role: be consistent. There's a tremendous amount of value in consistency, and that applies on many fronts. Be consistent in your priorities, in the way you treat people, and in your requirements about the delivery of projects.

Some say, "It's good to be inconsistent, because people never know what's coming, so they're always on their toes." But in fact, people need to have a good sense of who you are, what you're about, what your priorities are, and the way they need to interact with you. Consistency will enable them to communicate better with you and deliver your priorities.

It's also important to know your people. This goes beyond their names and job descriptions. Do you need to become best friends with them? No, but you need to understand what's going on in their personal lives, at least to some degree. Some

> **Key Requirements for Managers**
> 1. Consistency
> 2. Knowing your people
> 3. Confidence
> 4. Communication
> 5. Accountability
> 6. Support

argue that personal life and professional life are separate—period, end of story—but it's not really that way. If you have a bad day at work, you bring it home. If you have a bad day at home, you bring it to work. Knowing what people are going through and what's going on in their lives can help you understand why they're acting the way they do and what drives them.

What are their priorities? What's important to them? For one person, the priority may be upward mobility in the company. They want to get to work early, work hard, and work late. They don't care; they just want to get ahead. They want to get bonuses, raises, promotions. For other people, their real issue is balancing work and home. They're not as worried about raises and promotions. It's not that they're not interested in doing a great job, it's just that their motivation is a nice balance between work and home.

You've got to treat these two people differently. This is not to say that you should treat one better than the other. But because their motivations are different, how you interact with them is going to be different.

If someone is having a problem at home or going through a divorce or has a sick child, whether you'd like to admit it or not, these things will influence your day-to-day business. So it's a good idea to have some idea of what's going on with your people. It will make you a much more effective manager. It will make your staff more effective. Everybody will benefit, because you'll know how to interact with them, when to push, and when to back off.

Confidence is another important characteristic of a good manager. You need to exude a certain level of confidence. If you're wishy-washy, your staff will lose respect for you, and they won't be confident, because you're not. If you're weak and wishy-washy, they will reflect that. If you're strong and confident, your staff will reflect that as well.

You've got to be careful. Your staff is looking to you for leadership, whether they admit it or not. They're going to follow your lead; there is a feeling of following the leader.

A related point: you've often heard, "Don't sweat the small stuff." In management, the opposite is true: *do* sweat the small stuff. Be careful about ignoring little issues, because they tend to become big issues.

Communication is another key concept. The most important thing in communication is simply to communicate. Always communicate. Some managers feel, "I'm the boss; there are things that I have to keep private. I don't really want to give them out to my staff. I don't want them to know too much."

This attitude is wrong. Keeping your staff in the dark is a great demotivator. It keeps them wondering what's going on.

Management Styles and General Management

Rumors are much worse than reality. The level of distortion is like the telephone game. But in this case, you're not even telling them anything; they're just trying to guess at what's going on. What people can guess is amazing. Don't keep them in the dark. Give them an idea of what's going on. Don't let rumors overshadow reality.

Communicate often, daily, with your team members. This is why smaller teams are easier and function better: the leader can engage with the associates on a daily or weekly basis more often than those who have larger teams.

Empower your staff for accountability. Empower them to communicate, and when they do, reward them; when they don't, discuss it with them. If their failure to communicate has a negative impact on the team, explain that to them.

Encourage assertive communication. Be direct as possible without being abusive. Indirect communication results in missed deadlines, frustration, conflict, and confrontation. And certainly do not belittle or intimidate people. Use eye contact. Speak for yourself. Don't speak for others.

Be supportive of your people. The more successful your staff is, the more successful your department is, and the more successful you are. It's not about you being the best or being better than your staff. It's about teaching and mentoring them and helping them improve. The better they are, the better your department will be, and in the end, the better you will be. It's in your best interest to be supportive of your staff.

It's in your best interest to be supportive of your staff.

Getting Started

Now let's talk about a few things that you should deal with when you are getting started. To begin with, make sure you define your expectations. This goes beyond your expectations of your staff, your boss's expectations of you, and the company's expectations of each department.

It will help you a great deal to sit down and write out what you see as the expectations, whether you do this in longhand with a pen and paper or on a computer. Then talk about these expectations with your boss. Talk to colleagues in other departments to get their expectations of your department. Talk to your staff about what they expect from the job, from you, and from the company. Understand everybody's expectations. You have a much better chance of achieving your expectations than if you never bother to define them.

Once you've defined expectations, you need to manage them. Manage your staff's expectations about what can be done. Someone may define the expectations in your department in a way that's not really accurate. At this point, you have to go about trying to manage—and when necessary, change—your staff's expectations. Defining expectations gets you started, but you need to start managing them on an ongoing basis. That includes dealing with unrealistic expectations rather than ignoring them.

When you're getting started in a new role, you will also need to evaluate the team's abilities. There are always specific job descriptions, where everybody has a list of their expected tasks. Is it always that simple? No. Once people start working together in a team environment, everybody ends up starting to support one another. One person does a little bit more than their normal job, because they're good at it; another person performs a few different tasks, because that's what they're good at.

People don't fit together perfectly like dominoes, where the edges are smooth and they slide together. It's more like building a puzzle where everybody tends to go over their boundaries a little.

People end up overlapping and meshing together. You've got to evaluate your team from that perspective, not just to see what they're supposed to be doing, but what they actually *are* doing.

That runs into the next topic: responsibilities. What are people's responsibilities? As we've just seen, when you evaluate your team, it's not black-and-white; it's not just what's on their job description. People tend to adapt to their environment and take on or avoid responsibilities depending on their interests and capacities.

Get organized. In the past, you did your job. Now as a supervisor, you have to both do your job and be responsible for people doing their jobs—that is, management. You need to be able to get organized and keep everything under control. What that means is different for everybody. How you do it— whether you use calendars, to-do lists, Microsoft Outlook, or a handwritten portfolio—is specific to the individual. Everybody handles it differently. It's amazing how many people use so many different methods for task management. In the end, none of them is any better than the others. It's really about whether or not a given system works for you.

Working with Your Staff

Here in your role, it's time to manage your people. Let's get specific about a fairly common scenario: how do you handle a staff member who applied for the job that you've just gotten? Maybe both of you were coworkers in the same department, you both applied for the job, and you got it, or maybe you're coming in from the outside, whether it be outside the department or outside the company. In any case, one of the people working for you applied for your job but didn't get it.

In this situation, there's going to be a natural tendency for some resentment or defensiveness. Their reasons for why they should have gotten the job could be valid or invalid, but it doesn't really matter: they're upset.

In the best-case scenario, this person is reasonable and recognizes that you should have gotten the job over them for whatever reason, whether it be experience, seniority, knowledge, or working better with people. Maybe this person will say, "I can see why you are going to be more effective in this role than me." The worst-case scenario is when they try to undermine you at every point, whether consciously or subconsciously.

When you come in, you need to address this situation and assess where you are. Is this person somebody who is reasonable and understands why this happened,? Or are they unreasonable, and they're going to be a problem for you? Or are they somewhere in the middle?

This is not an easy situation to deal with. This is why managing people is a skill that a lot of people work hard to develop and maintain every day. People are different, so how you deal with them has to be different. Here are some tips.

You should meet with this person informally. Having them come into your office or a conference room for this discussion will reemphasize that you got the job and they didn't. If you were to take them out to lunch and have an informal discussion, you have a much better chance. It's a matter of getting through their defense mechanisms and having a real chat with them.

At this point, you have to figure out what's driving this person. Are they upset about money? Are they upset about recognition? What bothers them apart from the simple fact that you got the job and they didn't?

You can then use that knowledge to deal with the situation. If you are dealing with someone who is in the middle between best-case and worst-case scenarios, get them involved and bring them in. Make them part of the solution. Give them a voice. Don't give them control. Don't relinquish control to them, but bring them in as a confidant. Bring them in and tell them, "I value your opinion. I want you involved. I need you involved." Then follow up with real actions. Don't use empty words. You are going to end up damaging yourself and the department if you make promises you can't keep or if you say, "Yes, I want your involvement," and then you ignore them.

Another scenario is where you are working as a supervisor, and some of your subordinates are people who are your friends. Maybe you were working together, and you got this promotion and you went from being their coworker to being their boss.

These people may try to use your friendship to get the best projects or the best hours, or they can resent you for being their boss now. You have to work with them to figure out where you are. It's not that you can't be friends with your subordinates, but you do have to draw a line, and everybody knows where it is. Even so, they'll test the line to see what they can get away with. You have to be disciplined. You have to make sure you don't treat your friends any better than anybody else.

You also have to make sure you're not harder on your friends than on the rest of your staff. Some parents who coach sports are so worried about showing favoritism to their kids that they end up treating them worse than everybody else. The parent is so worried about showing favoritism to their own child that they go to the other extreme. You have to be careful of that in adult situations as well. You don't want to show favoritism, but you also don't want to be harder on this person than on anybody else. Be consistent and treat them just as you treat the rest of your staff.

You may also find yourself managing a staff member that has a grudge because they have more experience or are older than you. Here too, be consistent; treat them just like everybody else. You may want to bring them in a little closer. You may want to acknowledge and utilize that experience; make them an important part of the solution. As a matter of fact, these employees can turn into some of your greatest resources.

More of a standard configuration is working with a younger, more inexperienced staff member. Here you need to be their mentor. You need to educate them, train them, bring them along. As you do, the better and more experienced they will become at their job. That in turn will reflect well on you, your department, and the company.

The Power of Respect

When managing people, it's important to gain their respect. One question about management style has been around for years: is it better to be respected or feared? You can use the fear method: "Do what I say, or I'll write you up. Do what I say, or you're going to be fired." But today this style has become much less effective, if only because it's not so easy to fire someone anymore. In many cases that threat can prove to be empty: "I'll fire you." The employee can answer, "Well, go ahead and try," because in a lot of businesses, it's not easy to just decide that somebody needs to be fired.

> It's better to be respected than feared.

Let's go under the assumption that you are leaning more towards the idea of going with respect. But where does authority come from? Most people would tell you, "My boss. My boss hired me to be the supervisor, to be in charge, to be the authority figure. By this decree, he's giving me the authority to do what needs to be done within my job specs."

All this is true, but your authority doesn't come from your boss alone: it also comes from the mutual respect of everybody around you. People listen to you and act out your requests out of a certain level of respect. It's not just "I must do it, because if I don't, he'll write me up or she'll fire me." Now we're going back to authority by fear: "The boss said that, and he's the boss, so I have to listen to him." Yet if you go more on the respect avenue, you can get much more accomplished.

If authority comes from your boss, your staff can go to your boss to override your decisions. Do you really have the authority to manage your department? Not if your boss is undermining you. If the other department heads don't respect you and don't feel they can get things done with you, they can go directly to your boss or your subordinates. If your staff does things for other employees contrary to what you want, you've lost authority. Again, you are being undermined.

In short, gaining the respect of your subordinates, your boss, and your colleagues gives you your authority. In this case, your colleagues won't go to your subordinates, because your subordinates won't do anything unless it comes from you. They respect you and won't take action without your involvement.

The same is true with your boss and your colleagues. If your staff were to go to a colleague to get something done that clearly should have involved you, again your authority has been reduced. But if you have the respect of your boss, your subordinates, and your colleagues, you can maintain your authority and run the department the way you want it to run. Isn't that what it's all about? Because you're in charge, you need to run the department based on your priorities, and it will be successful or unsuccessful accordingly.

So how do you gain respect? As we've already seen, you need to be consistent. If people think you're inconsistent, they won't respect you. If you're acting differently from one day to the next, if your priorities shift from day to day, you start to lose respect.

Follow through on your commitments. If you say you're going to do something, do it. You can't blame your staff, because you're responsible for them. If you've made a commitment to a colleague or your boss and you assign the task to one of your staff members and they don't do it, that is your problem. It is a negative reflection on you, not your staff member, because it's your department. If you make a commitment, you've got to make sure to give the assignment to people who are going to get it done.

Make sure your commitments are followed through on, and accept responsibility for your own mistakes, whether they be your own or your staff's. In either case, you are responsible for the department. You've got to take responsibility for the mistakes that are made in your department and work to minimize those mistakes. Follow through; accept responsibility.

Another important point: don't be bossy. If you are walking around with a demeaning attitude and try to boss people around, people don't really respect that. Treat them with respect, and respect will come back your way. Treat people the way you want to be treated. If you're walking around with a haughty attitude, it will come back to you too.

Here is one possible approach. You don't say to your staff, "You need to get this done by five o'clock." You say, "Can you do me a favor and get this done by five o'clock?" Not everyone would agree with this attitude, but it will create an atmosphere where you'll make a request and your staff will deliver it out of mutual respect and a desire to work together. It's better than trying to rule with an iron fist.

This takes us back a point made earlier: you have to look at management styles and see which one fits you. Don't try to be somebody else who has a skill set that's different from yours; you won't be successful.

Also, gather feedback from all of those around you. Many people say, "I get an annual review. My boss tells me what he thinks of me. That's the feedback that I need, because he's the one that decides whether I get promoted or get a raise." But you can only learn so much from your boss, because they interact with you in a certain way. Your staff interacts with you in a different way, and your colleagues interact with you in yet another way. Feedback from all of these different vantage points will help you become a better manager.

Another point to keep in mind goes back to respect. People respect somebody who says, "I want to know what I'm doing well and what I'm not doing well, even though it's not a formal process. I want to know what I can do to improve." People respect that.

Managing People

It's often said, "Attitudes are catchy. Is yours worth catching?" This is a cliché, but clichés are often true. When you're a manager, people are looking at you, whether they admit it or not, whether they realize it or not, because you are the boss. They're looking up to you, especially if you follow the advice above: gaining their respect and treating them with respect and consistency. Your staff has a tendency to look up to you.

When you're a manager, people are looking at you.

What you allow to happen is what you are teaching your staff. If you allow them to be late every day, you're teaching them that it's OK to be late every day. If you're allowing them to deliver projects late all the time, you are teaching them it's OK to be late all the time on their projects.

You have to be careful of what you allow. Of course, there is a fine line between being respected and ruling with an iron fist. Saying, "I need you here at nine o'clock every morning" is not changing your management style to management by fear, because there are certain standards they need to adhere to. They need to know the guidelines and borders. This is true whether you're dealing with a five-year-old child or a fifty-year-old man. We all need to know where our boundaries are.

A related point is that your staff will do what you measure. Trust, but verify: "I trust that you are going to get your project done on time. But where are we right now? Are we on time? Are we behind?" If they know you're looking at that, they will be much more diligent about delivering on time. Many people—though not everybody—tend to be a little bit lax when they don't think anybody's looking. "The deadline is tomorrow, but no one's going to be checking. So is it OK to get it done in two or three days? It's not a big deal."

That's why you need to be diligent. What you measure is what your staff will do. If you're going to go to them tomorrow and say, "Where's the project? Is it done?" they're much more apt to get it done on time than if they think, "She might not even notice it's late."

Here's an example. Early in his career, a man was working in New York City when there was a horrible ice storm. Ice formed on the railroad tracks; it was a nightmare. He started early in the morning, but not so early that they were closing businesses. By nine or ten o'clock, it started to get really nasty. This man and three or four of his colleagues all showed up to work, but one called in and said, "I'm not feeling so good. I'm not sure I'm going to come into the office today."

About twelve o'clock, when they decided to shut the office down, the same employee called up and said, "You know what? I'm feeling better. I'm going to come in now." At that point, he was told not to bother.

This employee was not charged a sick day for being out. That affected the rest of the department, because their attitude was, "Why did I go through the hassle of getting up and trudging through the snow to make it into the office and then incur the expense and nightmare of trying to get out of New York City with the trains shut down? Why did I go through all that if I could have just said I'm sick and not even been charged a day?"

In short, that employee was rewarded for doing the wrong thing. The rest of the department felt, "You didn't reward me for coming in. I didn't get another day off. He got rewarded for not coming in."

You have to be careful about making mistakes like that. Again, it has to do with consistency. Some of the decisions you make for one person might demotivate the others.

People often equate rewards with money. But you can't always give bonuses or go in to your supervisors and say, "I want to give this guy an extra $500."

A number of studies, evaluating thousands of people, have been done on what motivates employees. Money is not even in the top five. A reward can be as simple as, "Great job." You can reward them with taking them out to lunch. You can reward them by sending out an email saying, "I just wanted to make sure everybody knows that Sally went way beyond her responsibilities to make sure we delivered this project on time." That's a reward mechanism, whether you realize it or not. When people see that you are rewarding them for going above and beyond their basic duties, that's what they'll continue to do.

There are other ways to reward employees. You can innovate in giving out different types of rewards. You can recognize the employee of the month. You see those all over the place. That's because, as corny as some people might think they are, they are effective.

What Do They Want?

Apart from rewards, what does your staff want from you, and what can you give them?

Employees generally want training and development. Most people want to improve and develop themselves, but sometimes they don't know what they need to do. That's part of your job as a manager: you need to train them to develop and improve.

Give your staff performance feedback, and not just once a year. You need to talk to people and give them feedback on a consistent basis. Are they doing well? Are they having problems? What do they need to improve? You should do that at least once a quarter. Some managers do it once a week.

This is not a formal process of filling out forms, but simply sitting down with a person and having a chat with them. You say, "I've noticed these things are going really well. I like the way you're handling this task, but I noticed over a couple of days you've been slipping on this other task. I'm not sure you understand how to handle that. Maybe you can take some time to work on it, or maybe you and I can get together tomorrow, and we'll go over how to do it a different way."

> Provide feedback, both positive and negative, on a regular basis.

Provide feedback, both positive and negative, on a regular basis. Use this ratio: For every one time you have to discipline or provide negative feedback, you should be providing positive feedback eight to ten times. The ratio is 8:1, or 10:1. If you're giving praise and negative feedback on a 50/50 basis, you're focusing on the wrong things. Try to find what people are doing right. This will keep their self-esteem high and increase their likelihood of success.

Second, although it should go without saying, your employees need effective management. They need you to keep things under control and manage the department. As we've already seen, this includes managing expectations. It also involves managing projects, administrative tasks, and simply getting the job done.

General Management

Once you take over as a supervisor, it's your responsibility not only to manage people, but to manage all of their actions, tasks, and projects. So we're going to talk a little bit more about general management now.

First is management by objectives: you want to clearly identify the objectives for the department (or the project or the company). People are able to maintain their focus when they know their objectives. Some of these may be generic and ongoing: things you need to do day in, day out, week by week, month by month. Others may be objectives for specific projects.

How do you create an objective? You can use the SMART approach. This is an acronym: S stands for *specific*. Your

---

The SMART Approach
- Specific
- Measurable
- Agreed upon (sometimes Achievable)
- Realistic
- Time framed

objective needs to be specific: "I'm going to accomplish X or Y." It also has to be *measurable*. Can you measure this objective? Can you show that it was a success or failure?

A: The objective also has to be *agreed upon*. This is not necessarily a matter of getting everybody to say, "We all agree that this is an objective we want." Rather, you need to have everybody agree to an understanding of the objective and what they're going to do with it. (In some models, A stands for *achievable*.)

R: The objective also has to be *realistic*. It's not productive to say you're going to get something accomplished in an unreasonable time frame or for an unreasonable amount of money. Everybody knows you're not going to hit these goals, so it doesn't allow them to maintain their focus. People will look at your objective and say, "That's not going to work anyway."

T: The objective also has to have a *time frame*.

Ongoing is not a time frame. Even when you have ongoing tasks, you need to set them in some kind of time context: "Our objective is to resolve a certain percentage of issues every week." Then you can determine how well you're doing: "How many issues have we resolved within one week?" Or you may say you are going to create a new manual for the department by the end of the year. That's a time frame. Whether it's realistic depends on what you expect from your new manual and what time of the year it is. In any event, it's specific, measurable, and agreed upon.

Now that you have the objectives (others might call them guidelines), you need to look at the work you have to do in order to accomplish them. You will need to delegate. This is one of the most difficult parts of management, especially when you're making the transition from staff to supervisor. Many managers who do so struggle with effective delegation. As a staff member, you had a project or a task, and you took care of it yourself. You didn't give it to somebody else to do.

But the precise job of a manager is to assign work to others to do. So how do you delegate, and what should be delegated? Here again, you have to be consistent, for example in assigning desirable and undesirable projects. Don't cherry-pick projects for yourself and only delegate the undesirable ones. That doesn't work well, because it becomes obvious. People start to be demotivated, because they feel that all you do is dump the garbage on them. You have to be fair and consistent in delegating tasks.

You also have to select the appropriate person for the task or project. You can't arbitrarily say, "This is your responsibility. Here's the project. You go do it." You can't match a project with somebody who doesn't have the right skills for it.

It's also critical to clearly communicate the what and why of the task. You can't assign a project without explaining what is expected—or why. Some will tell you that it doesn't really matter why: you're the boss; they're the subordinate; you tell them what to do, and that's it. Some parents act that way: "Don't ask *why?* Just do what I tell you to do."

But most people are inquisitive: they want to understand why they're doing a task. They want to understand the benefits of what they're doing and how it fits into everything else. This should make them more effective at what they're doing.

Understanding the *why* of the project can be extremely important. Say you're doing a task to improve security, but an employee who is working on it realizes that what they're doing doesn't improve security, but may even weaken it. Now they have a chance to come back to you and say, "I don't think this is going to work," or, "I have a problem here." Whereas if you leave out the why, they're just going to accomplish what you told them to do, regardless of whether it improves security or not.

You can't just give a project to somebody and walk away, saying, "It's your responsibility. You take care of it. Come back to me when it's done." You need to follow up with them. Because sometimes things get difficult, or people get distracted and they don't give the task the attention it deserves. If you're not following up, it's easy for them to put it on the back burner and ignore it until somebody cares.

Then give credit where credit is due. If you delegate something to an employee and they're successful at it, make sure you give them credit. It will always reflect positively on you if your staff does something positive. Don't be afraid that they will get the credit and you will be left in the shadows. Give them the credit. It makes you look better, because you have a successful staff member and successful department.

Why We Don't Delegate

Here are some common reasons why we don't delegate. These are the things to avoid.

Here's the first: "It's easier to do it myself. It will take me ten minutes. It will take me an hour and a half to teach them how to do it." Maybe, if it's a one-time task and you have the time; otherwise, that's a bad way to look at it. If this is an ongoing task that needs to be done every week, every month, or every year, and if it is something that a subordinate can do, you have to teach them.

It's your job to teach them and delegate that responsibility to them. Besides, if they can handle it, that frees you up.

Another thing people say is, "I can't trust them. It's my responsibility. I need to get it done myself." If you can't trust your staff, you have a problem. You need to be able to trust your staff to get things done. You need to be able to trust your staff to be smart enough, to be good enough at what they do, to take on these responsibilities. Yes, everything is your responsibility in that department, but you can't do it all yourself. This is why you have a staff. Get used to delegating.

If you have somebody you can't trust, you need to find a way to work with them or improve their skills so you *can* trust them. If this isn't possible, look at other options, whether it be moving the problematic employee to another department or firing them.

The next one: "I can't keep track of them." It's your job to keep track of your staff. You need to be able to delegate tasks to them and keep track of what's going on. That is your responsibility as a supervisor.

Another excuse: "What if they do it better than me?" You'd be lucky if they did it better than you, because that's part of the whole point of how a team functions. We are not all created equal. We don't all have the same skill sets. A successful department will have people who do some things better than their supervisor; some departments will have many people doing things better than their supervisor. This is certainly the case in information technology (IT). There's the jack-of-all-trades, who understands technology and how they all fit together. Then there are specialists, such as people who know database servers. You as a manager can never go as deep as they do, because you have other responsibilities. It would be a great thing if your staff did things better than you. It reflects well on them, on you, and on the department.

One classic in the management field is *Seven Habits of Highly Effective People*, by Stephen R. Covey. He delves into the concept of delegation. He warns against being two types of delegator.

The first type is the gofer dumper, aka the micromanager. In other words, they are working on the overall project and they say, "You go get me this. You go do that." They give out little individual tasks for people to do rather than giving them the project along with the responsibility to get things done. They manage every little detail.

The other type of delegator that he warns against is the seagull. The seagull delegator floats around, keeps an eye on things, flies in, dumps a load of work on your desk, and says, "Here, get this done." Seagulls just dump and fly off. There's very little interaction or communication as the task progresses.

The seagull resembles the hands-off manager, who makes no effort to integrate. You may think, "It sounds great; I would love my boss to just give me what I've got to do and leave me alone." In some cases it is, but in other cases it becomes very inefficient and ineffective. If you have a boss that doesn't contact you for weeks on end, that's too long, because you need to understand the larger picture. The boss is involved in things that you're not. You need to know what's going on, but you're getting no information from your boss. The ideal manager is a delicate balance between a micromanager and a dumper.

> The ideal manager is a delicate balance between a micromanager and a dumper.

Time Management

Everybody needs to manage time:, supervisor, manager, director, vice president, CEO, everyday staff. Everybody needs effective time management. Fred Pryor and Career Track have a number of titles related to this subject, and you may want to look at some of them. Here let's do a quick synopsis of time management.

To begin with, make sure you eliminate unnecessary tasks. Look at the things that you really don't need to be doing and stop doing them.

Next, you need to make lists, whether it be on pen and paper or on the computer. Most people can't keep track of everything that is bombarded on them, from emails, meetings, or hallway conversation or in a meeting. So many tasks or projects are being brought up that you need to make lists to track it all and focus on the priorities.

You also need to take breaks. You cannot work for twelve hours straight without reducing your effectiveness. It may seem like a badge of honor to say, "I worked eighteen hours today." Nevertheless, you need to take a break and back away, even for as little as ten or fifteen minutes, to let your brain calm down and give yourself a better perspective.

There are many approaches to priority management. A simple one is called Eat That Frog. In this case, the "frog" is the most important task you have at hand that, for whatever reason, you avoid. The solution is simple: eat the frog: do the task that you're most resisting *first*. Get the hard task done first, because you're going to have no problem doing the ones that you want to do. The tasks that you avoid like the plague will come back to bite you.

Key Points in This Chapter

Let's take a look at what we've covered in this chapter. We've talked about the different management styles and how they might fit with your personality or skill set and how a combination of different styles might be really what you're looking for.

Then we looked at some tips for getting started. We looked into managing people in different ways, because each person is different. It's important to get to know your people. The better you know them, the better you'll know how to manage and motivate them and how to get things done.

Finally, we looked at general management, project management, and task and priority management. Some of these, such as the latter two, are vital for all employees but especially so for supervisors.

TWO

How to Avoid the Most Common Mistakes

New managers are often promoted for their expertise, work ethic, and ability to get work done. They may have demonstrated leadership potential as a result of the relationships they have built with their coworkers. You learn how to be a good and effective manager through experience, coaching, and mentorship.

You can avoid the most common mistakes new managers make. We'll review five topics:
- Know your job.
- Focus on the right things.
- Know your team members.
- Lead your team.
- Manage yourself.

Know Your Job

As a manager, it is your responsibility to collaborate with each individual and with the team to establish goals. These goals should support the department and the organization's vision and/or mission. The goals will inform who is responsible for the work that needs to be done to accomplish the overall objectives. It is your responsibility to ensure that the work gets done. This means organizing and assigning the tasks that need to be completed. Training and development of your team ensures that they are capable of performing their jobs to the best of their ability and prepares them for growth within the organization.

Employee engagement should be a manager's primary role. As the manager, you're responsible for holding your team and the individuals accountable for delivering results. You will do this by setting measurable targets and expectations and regularly reviewing the results with your team.

Finally, there are administrative duties, which will vary based on your industry. These are tasks like preparing schedules, processing payroll, conducting performance reviews, and managing a budget.

Ten Big Mistakes

Let's discuss ten of the most common mistakes new managers make when it comes to knowing their job.

1. **Failing to delegate.** As we've already seen, new managers often get caught in the trap of doing rather than organizing the work. It is now your responsibility to assign tasks and motivate the team to accomplish its goals and objectives. Be sure to focus on the what and not the how.
2. **Managing work instead of leading people.** Yes, your new title is manager. Successful managers strive to be

> **Ten Management Mistakes**
> 1. Failing to delegate
> 2. Managing work instead of leading people
> 3. Believing you need to know everything
> 4. Acting too quickly or too slowly
> 5. Not knowing when to be discreet
> 6. Taking sides
> 7. Confusing authority with power
> 8. Failing to take responsibility for results
> 9. Waiting too long to address staffing concerns
> 10. Failing to learn and train your team

leaders. Let go of controlling every task. Give your team room to perform their job duties and build relationships. Motivate your team to perform. Avoid dictating what needs to be done and how to do it. Work *with* your team versus having them work for you.

3. **Believing you need to know everything.** Avoid acting as though you know—or need to know—everything. If you listen to people and ask questions, you will learn. Keep an open mind. You don't have to take every piece of advice that you're given. Just be open to hearing people out. Don't think that you'll impress your boss by acting as if you don't need help. Every job—including the one you had before you were promoted—is to help your boss get the job done and achieve the company's goals. Budget time to meet with your boss to give information and get guidance and mentoring. Be eager to learn from your boss and your team.

> You don't need to know everything.

4. **Acting too quickly or too slowly.** Take the time to know the processes, procedures, rules, and policies before you change anything. No need to reinvent the wheel: see what works and what doesn't work before you start making changes. Strive to always be curious.
5. **Not knowing when to be discreet.** Discretion goes two ways: (1) Knowing what information you are privy to as a manager that should not be shared with your team. (2) Keeping the confidence of your team members. As they learn to trust you, they will confide in you more and more. Only take action if it's necessary; otherwise, keep their confidence. Coach, advise, and encourage staff to solve their own problems. When they share something with you that requires you to act, tell them your intentions. If you are unsure what company information can be shared, ask your boss or another leader.
6. **Taking sides.** This is definitely going to happen from time to time: an employee will try to use you and your authority to win a dispute with a coworker. Do not act based on an employee's complaint without checking the facts. Conduct your own investigation. Maintain your objectivity.
7. **Confusing authority with power.** Do not mistake authority for power. Understand the authority that comes with your new position. Know that influence is much more

powerful than authority and that you earn trust and respect. Leaders influence regardless of their position or authority. People who merely work for managers are likely to do the minimum required. People follow leaders. When your team knows, likes, and trusts you, they will be more productive and will consistently perform at a higher level. Earn their trust and respect, and your team will be more engaged, motivated, and productive.

8. **Failing to take responsibility for results.** As the manager, you are responsible for your own results and the results of your team. If your team fails, you have failed. Avoid blaming your team or any member of your team. Take each failure as a learning experience. Work with the team to overcome failures and prevent making the same mistakes in the future. Focus on what happened, not on who did it.

9. **Waiting too long to address staffing concerns.** Even the most experienced managers wish there were a magic formula for finding and hiring the right people. It is hard. Do whatever you can to research your candidates and find people who will be a good fit for the job and the team. Consider keeping a short list of candidates for the various positions on your team so you're ready when you have a vacancy. When an employee is not working out, don't wait too long before taking action (even though this is the least enjoyable aspect of being a manager). Determine the steps necessary to improve their performance, or encourage them to move on. It will get worse the longer you avoid acting. Your goal is to fire fast and hire slow.

10. **Failing to continue to learn and train your team.** Even the most experienced and talented employees need training, and that need does not go away. Failure to learn the value of training for yourself and your employees is a costly mistake. People who are up-to-date on the newest technologies are more productive and feel more confident to do a better job. Value lifelong learning and continual improvement. As a manager, you will benefit from training, even when it's a refresher. If your budget is limited, utilize your key people to share their tips and experience with others, and consider using the expertise of individuals in other departments. Establish a culture of intentional learning. This is a strategy to retain and attract the best talent.

The Skills of Intentional Learners

The global consulting firm McKinsey and Company has shared five core skills of intentional learners.
1. **Set small, clear goals** and take a once-in-a-career approach when faced with exceptionally challenging situations.
2. **Remove distractions** and protect time for learning.
3. **Seek actionable feedback** to identify your blind spots. You don't know they're there: that's why they're blind spots. Feedback from your team, your peers, and your boss will help you to discover them.
4. **Practice deliberately.** Experts are made, not born.
5. **Practice reflection** before, during, and after a task.

> **Five Core Skills of Intentional Learners**
> 1. Set small, clear goals.
> 2. Remove distractions.
> 3. Seek actionable feedback.
> 4. Practice deliberately.
> 5. Practice reflection.

Follow these techniques for intentional learning, and teach them to your team. You'll all benefit.

Focus on the Right Things

As an employee, you focused on tasks, responding to requests, completing projects, and other duties as they were assigned to you. As a manager, it is your responsibility to keep your focus on the bigger picture: the mission and vision of the organization. As you strive to accomplish this mission, it is also your responsibility to work within the organization's guidelines and ensure your team does the same. This means ensuring you are compliant with government rules and regulations. You are also responsible for setting and meeting the goals and objectives of your position and your department. You will accomplish all of this by working with your team.

Let's review the ten major mistakes new managers make when it comes to focusing on the right things.

1. **Forgetting about the big picture.** People often concentrate on how and what they do without any knowledge of the impact of what they do or how it benefits the

organization as a whole. Your employees will be more engaged and motivated if they know that their day-to-day tasks are contributing to something bigger than themselves. As humans, our greatest fear is to live a meaningless life. Understanding the impact and the why behind our responsibilities ties our work to the bigger picture. Ensure that both you and each of your team members know the impact of what you do on the organization as a whole. It is a great motivator to know that your work is an important contribution to the organization.

2. **Avoiding problems.** A manager's primary responsibility is to solve problems. This means being available to your team and ensuring that they know they can bring their problems and challenges to you. You've heard about the open-door policy: this means the door is open more than it is closed. As you support your team in resolving problems and challenges, they will become more confident in resolving them on their own. Be careful to avoid punishing the messenger for mistakes. If you do, your team will not trust you. They will end up hiding problems and mistakes from you. This will result in unpleasant surprises down the road that could have been avoided with an open-door policy.

3. **Losing focus on your responsibilities.** Once you've committed to an open-door policy, it is important to avoid taking on all the problems and challenges that your team brings to you. The goal is to coach and support them as they find solutions and work to a resolution. Let your staff know that they can come to you with problems or potential problems and with suggestions on how to improve

> **Ten Mistakes in Managerial Focus**
> 1. Forgetting about the big picture
> 2. Avoiding problems
> 3. Losing focus on your responsibilities
> 4. Focusing on *who* rather than *what*
> 5. Not admitting mistakes
> 6. Not respecting human resources (HR) rules and guidelines
> 7. Not investing in relationships
> 8. Making decisions too quickly
> 9. Focusing on the perks of your position
> 10. Taking all the credit

the process. But don't let them just dump the problem on you and leave. Help them figure out a solution.

4. **Focusing on *who* rather than *what*.** Have you ever been in a situation where everyone involved in discussing a problem is spending all of their time trying to figure out who is to blame rather than how to resolve that problem? This behavior prevents the team from discovering a resolution and often leads to conflict and confrontation. Focus on attacking the problem, not the person or people involved. Keep the attention on how to resolve it and prevent it from happening again. This may mean more training and improved communications. Everyone involved should take some responsibility for the problem without blaming any one person. As a manager, if you focus on the problem rather than placing blame, your

team will trust you and they will learn how to solve problems on their own. Foster an attitude that says, "Hey, this is where we are. What can we do to fix this?" This way, people won't try to hide the cause of the problem for fear that they will get in trouble.

5. **Not admitting mistakes.** If you want your employees to feel comfortable and safe when admitting mistakes, it's up to you to set the example. When you make a mistake, admit it. You can say something like, "Here's what happened," and add, "I am responsible for this." Then add, "I'm sharing this with you so that we can all learn from my mistake." This is likely to significantly improve relationships with employees. Be sincere as you admit your mistakes. You'll come across as a strong leader. Your team will know that they can admit to mistakes instead of making excuses for them, and you'll be seen as just a little more human.

6. **Not respecting human resources (HR) rules and guidelines.** This is very important. Your employees have rights, and there are laws and regulations in place to protect them. Your HR professionals are well-versed in these, but it's still your responsibility to be familiar with them and discuss any concerns with your HR person. Many managers don't know the rules, so they put the organization and themselves at risk, since both can be held accountable though legal action when the regulations are not followed. If you have an HR department, work with them. Don't just dump your employee management responsibilities on HR. Be educated and know what your rights are as a manager as well as your employees' rights. Treat your HR department as a partner.

> Your employees have rights, and there are laws and regulations in place to protect them.

7. **Not investing in relationships.** If you work in an organization with several departments, rivalries are likely to develop. Your goal is to avoid them. You need to do your job so that the next department can do theirs. Have you ever found yourself in a position where you had to wait on another department or another person, feeling as though they were slowing down the process or using more than their fair share of the resources, and as a result, you are concerned about making your own deadlines? This happens everywhere. As satisfying as it might seem to complain about other departments or other people, blaming your peers for slowdowns and poor results will likely backfire on you. To ensure the best outcome, build relationships and cooperate to get the best results for all involved. You and your team will come out on top.

   Here's a real-life case: a manager was responsible for a loyalty department for a hospitality company. The manager and two other peers used significant resources from the IT department. The manager's team prided themselves on being good partners with the technology group. They would take over coffee and donuts when meeting with them and work with them to deal with bugs and challenges. They would look at each situation and determine what was most important for the organization overall. The loyalty department did not put themselves first.

Another manager did not take that approach. He always wanted him, his team, and his responsibilities to come first. He behaved like a rival to IT and his peers. He complained quite a bit about IT, and he had some very loud conversations with the leadership in that area.

A few years into the job, the manager of the loyalty department was one-on-one with the chief technology officer. He had a slush fund, as he called it, of about $400,000 in discretionary dollars and was able to choose what projects to apply those funds towards. He informed the loyalty department manager that this particular year he had determined that he was going to use the entire $400,000 to support the initiatives of this manager's group. He said he had chosen this team and its projects because they were partners with his team. He wanted to reward this department for building strong relationships with IT. Those relationships and that partnership helped this department come out on top.

8. **Making decisions too quickly.** As a manager, you have to make decisions all the time, and from the outside at times it might look as if you are making abrupt decisions. If you must give a quick answer, make decisions based on the best information that you have available at that time. For important decisions, implement a decision-making strategy and go through a logical process to make the best decisions that you can with the information available.

Here's an example of a decision-making strategy. Ask yourself these questions: Am I part of the problem or the solution? Do I need to solve it, or is there someone better? If it is not your problem, let the person who owns the problem solve it. You can support them along the way. Determine the root cause of the problem and involve others in problem-solving. This will enable your team and peers to trust your decision-making.

9. **Focusing on the perks of your position.** As a manager, you have perks that come with your position that your employees do not have. By all means take advantage of these perks, but it is a mistake to brag about them. Remember what it would have felt like when you were on the other side of the equation. Don't act in any way that you would resent from a boss.

10. **Taking all the credit.** A good manager takes the blame and shares the credit. Your performance will be assessed based on the accomplishments of your staff. Take every opportunity to give credit to your team and to the individuals involved. Do this often, and do it publicly. Take advantage of your employee recognition programs to ensure that your team members' contributions are seen and celebrated. Mistakes that become visible outside of your department are on you. You are responsible for the work and the mistakes of your team. Take the blame and share the credit.

Know Your Team Members

This is a point we've covered already, but it is extremely important. Know your employees; know them personally; know their strengths, weaknesses, and personality styles.

Treat everyone fairly and adjust your approach based on the individual. Set clear goals and expectations for each person on your team. Be a far better listener than you are a talker.

Let's take a look at the ten mistakes new managers make when it comes to knowing your team members.

1. **Treating everyone the same.** You might have some training in management techniques. They won't work the same with every one of your employees. Each of them is different, with different personality types and different work and learning styles. It would be a good idea to learn about personality types and situational leadership techniques to help you see your employees as individuals.

2. **Not treating everyone equally.** Treating employees equally is not equivalent to treating everyone the same. At some point, you will have an employee accuse you of unfair treatment. It may be the result of negative feedback, an undesirable assignment, or a disciplinary measure, and the employee doesn't like it. They may decide that you are not being fair and not treating them equally. Your best defense against this is to treat all of your employees fairly. Document your reasons for negative feedback or discipline, and be prepared to defend those actions.

3. **Showing favoritism.** You may be managing some friends that you worked with in your old position. They are the people you will feel most comfortable with. Avoid showing favoritism to them. This will only breed resentment towards you and your favorites. Treat every one of your employees equally, and be sure not to show favoritism to any.

> **Ten Mistakes in Knowing Employees**
> 1. Treating everyone the same
> 2. Not treating everyone equally
> 3. Showing favoritism
> 4. Striving to be liked
> 5. Prioritizing tasks over people
> 6. Failing to set clear goals and expectations
> 7. Ignoring problems
> 8. Expecting staff to earn your trust
> 9. Not being open to ideas from the team
> 10. Not knowing employees' strengths and weaknesses

4. **Striving to be liked.** Everyone wants to be liked: that is perfectly normal. But every manager finds out sooner or later that someone doesn't like them. It is a waste of your time and energy to focus on being liked by everyone: it will keep you from being productive and effective. People will like you or they won't. Concentrate on being fair and treating your employees equally. If you do that, you've done all that you can.

5. **Prioritizing tasks over people.** You have a lot of administrative responsibilities, a budget to write, spreadsheets to analyze, reports to review. You are always behind on email—and let's not forget all those meetings you're expected to attend. Your most important responsibility is to get a team of people to work together to accomplish specific goals. You can't do that without making time for

them. Be friendly and approachable. Take a few moments to chat with different team members throughout the day. When you have a meeting with an employee, show them that it is the most important thing you have on your schedule at that moment. Turn off your devices and give that person your undivided attention. If you're meeting with them virtually, close other applications to avoid distraction. If someone else comes into your office, let them know that you're in an important meeting and you'll speak with them later.

Be friendly and approachable.

It is essential to have a good system for prioritizing everything you need to get done in a day, week, and month. Management consultant Brian Tracy prioritizes everything based on a system of A, B, C, D, or E.

A is for the most important tasks: things that you *must* get done.

B is for tasks and projects that have minor consequences if they're not done. These are things that you *should* do.

C stands for items for which there are absolutely no consequences. These are the "nice to dos."

D marks the items and projects and tasks that you can *delegate* to others.

E stands for *elimination*. When you take a look at your list and some items on it have been on it for months or even years, consider eliminating them altogether. If you haven't done them by now, they most likely are not important and don't have any consequences at all.

6. **Failing to set clear goals and expectations.** Managers assume that their employees know what is expected. Your employees need to know what you expect them to do. They also need to know what success looks like. It sounds simple, but it is an area of extremely common mistakes. Clearly communicate expectations and then check. Ask the employee to articulate their understanding of the goal and then ask them to articulate what success looks like. If they're not able to meet the goal, repeat the goals and expectations, ask them again what success looks like, and have them try again.

7. **Ignoring problems.** Employee problems are not going to get better until you take action. If you have a problem employee, it is essential that you take steps to resolve it. Whether it is a concern about performance or discipline, you must be prepared to have those tough conversations and work towards solutions. Putting it off will only make it worse.

8. **Expecting staff to earn your trust.** As a manager, you have as your goal earning the trust of your team. If they trust you, they will follow you. If you expect them to earn your trust, they will hesitate in trusting you. Take the approach that every employee is worthy of your trust until proved otherwise. Although you may get the occasional employee who will take advantage of this, there are processes for handling employees who do things that they should not.

9. **Not being open to ideas from the team.** Managers often ask their employees for opinions and ideas and then ignore them. If you're going to ignore them, why bother asking? Take the time to listen intently to your employees' input and ideas and give them serious consideration.
10. **Not knowing employees' strengths and weaknesses.** You should know the strengths and weaknesses of your employees and how you can leverage their abilities to accomplish your department's objectives. Identify each individual's sweet spot: where their passion and skills overlap with the needs of the organization. Each team member should be doing work that they are good at and have a passion for. They will end up enjoying the work more and they will make a bigger impact on the overall results.

You can also consider using a SWOT analysis to determine the best possible use of your employees' abilities. SWOT stands for *strengths, weaknesses, opportunities,* and *threats*. Include each team member in the preparation of their SWOT analysis. Consider making this a quarterly process. It will help inform opportunities to leverage their abilities and will also identify areas for further development. Again, every employee is an individual, and one size doesn't fit all. If you learn this technique, you will be able to manage your employees as individuals.

SWOT Analysis

- Strengths
- Weaknesses
- Opportunities
- Threats

Ten Leadership Mistakes

Be clear about your goals and objectives as a manager. If you are unclear, ask questions, and meet with your new boss regularly to get clarification.

Here are ten mistakes new managers make when leading their teams.

1. Failing to transition to manager.

Many managers like their old job so much that they keep doing it after they are promoted to management. To be successful, you must let go of that comfort zone. If you think of your old job as the real work and your management responsibilities as something that is getting in the way of getting the real work done, you will never be an effective manager. Your job is now getting the work done through the people on your team. This is going to require new skills. It also requires letting go of your old responsibilities.

2. Failing to delegate.

Delegation is a skill. Like most skills, it will require practice. The most common barriers to delegating are not wanting to lose control and the belief that the other person will not do it right or that you can do it better. The more technical the job, the more likely you are to struggle with letting go. But it is important to delegate not only menial and rudimentary tasks, but meaningful work that enables employees to learn and grow. A good guideline is to delegate a task or project when the person is 80 percent capable of completing it. Establish regular

> **Ten Mistakes in Team Leadership**
> 1. Failing to transition to manager
> 2. Failing to delegate
> 3. Failing to motivate
> 4. Acting when it is not necessary or appropriate
> 5. Sending mixed messages
> 6. Not sharing the why
> 7. Not protecting team members
> 8. Unproductive meetings
> 9. Not recognizing accomplishments
> 10. Not conducting employee evaluations

check-ins. Do not micromanage every step along the way. Delegate the result, not the *how*. You must give your employees something to own. Delegate a function, not just errands.

Let's look at the five levels of delegation.

Level 1. "Do as I say." "Do what I've asked or told you to do. Don't deviate." This is not ideal. Employees at this level will feel micromanaged.

Level 2. Your employee researches the topic, gathers information, and reports to you on what they have discovered. You discuss it together and you make the decision together. This level gives you an opportunity to test their decision-making skills.

Level 3. The employee has proven their ability to come up with solutions. You are trusting them to outline the options and bring their best recommendation. If you agree with their findings and decision, you authorize them to move forward.

> **Five Levels of Delegation**
> 1. "Do as I say."
> 2. Employee gathers information and discusses it with supervisor, and the two decide together on a plan of action.
> 3. The employee outlines the options and makes their best recommendation.
> 4. The employee reviews information, chooses a plan of action, and implements it, keeping the supervisor informed.
> 5. The employee makes whatever decision they think is best with no obligation to report back.

Level 4. The employee has proven their ability to decide on a solution, choose a plan of action, and implement it. You allow them to make decisions and then tell you what they did. You trust them to do the research, make the best decision they can, and keep you in the loop.

Level 5. You trust the employee to make whatever decision they think is best, with no need to report back. At this level, you are demonstrating your trust in the employee, as they have risen from one level to the next. They have demonstrated their ability to manage tasks and complete them. They are fully accountable for the outcome. They know what to do and they know they can do it. There's one caveat: no surprises.

3. Failing to motivate.

Get training in this area. There are many ways to motivate employees. Again, each of your employees is an individual, and no single type of motivation will work for them all. Recall management responsibility number 4: employee engagement and motivation, which should be a manager's primary responsibility. Don't expect people to motivate themselves: it is your job. Managers often fail to let their employees know how they fit into the bigger picture and contribute to the organization's mission. It is essential to help each person see how they contribute to that bigger picture.

If you are not motivated, your team will not be motivated. Be a good example. Be the leader. You set the pace for the team. Review your attitude and behavior. Are you motivated? If not, work on your own motivation first, then work on that of your team.

4. Acting when it is not necessary or appropriate.

Sometimes the best action is no action at all. You do not have to be involved in everything. You do not have to solve every problem. Know when to leave it to your team to resolve issues.

5. Sending mixed messages.

Employees are paying attention not only to what you say but also to what you do. Most of what they learn from their managers is what they observe, not what they hear. Be conscious of your actions and ensure that they are aligned with your values. If you expect people to be on time to meetings, always be on time. (Being on time means being a few—say five—minutes early.) The standards you model are the standards your team will abide by; the standards you ignore, they will ignore. Your team will follow your lead, your actions, and your behavior. Most essentially, avoid the attitude of "Do as I say, not as I do."

6. Not sharing the why.

Employees will be more responsive and responsible when they understand the why behind what you expect of them. When given tasks and assignments that require apparently unproductive or confusing procedures, an employee is likely to think, "What's in it for me?" or "How does this affect me?" This is human nature. When explaining a process, share the why and explain how it impacts the organization's mission or the customer. Your employees will be more likely to follow procedures and policies when they understand the why behind them. When you explain the reasons, they will feel that they are being consulted and informed rather than merely ordered to do something.

A good leader shares the credit and takes the blame.

---

7. Not protecting team members.

A good leader shares the credit and takes the blame. Protect your team from outside influences that may impede their ability to do their jobs. Make it as easy as possible for your team to get their work done. Make it clear to them that blame is on you. Doing so will engender loyalty that will compensate for the rough time you may experience when protecting your people.

8. Unproductive meetings.

Learn how to make meetings productive. Meeting management is a skill that can be learned. Consider getting some training in meeting management.

Here are five tips for conducting productive meetings:
- Consider the best day and time of day to have the meeting.
- Reward punctuality.
- Prepare the agenda in advance and share it.
- Communicate the objective in advance.
- Eliminate all unnecessary meetings. If there is no reason for the meeting, why have it?

Your team and your peers will appreciate you for respecting their time. If the information shared in the meeting can be shared effectively in email, do not hold the meeting.

9. Not recognizing accomplishments.

Consider the employee first before deciding how to recognize them. It should take place in public unless the person does not like public recognition. Never praise somebody for average or mediocre work: if you do, you're going to get more mediocre work.

10. Not conducting employee evaluations.

Performance evaluations are time-consuming, and they are hard work. They require advanced preparation, recordkeeping, and note taking throughout the year. Even so, one of your greatest responsibilities as a manager is to provide your employees with feedback on their performance: it is a key strategy for motivating and retaining your best talent. Your employees deserve to know how you think they're doing. If you feel they need improvement, they need to know this too. An employee with ambition to grow at the organization will need your feedback, which is essential to improve their performance, increase their salary, and be considered for advancement. Strive to provide equal portions of constructive feedback and praise. Ensure that your employees know what they are doing right so they can do more of it. Give continual feedback, so that there are no surprises when you sit down for an evaluation. If your company requires an annual performance review, this is of course essential. A best practice is to meet with each of your direct reports no less than once a month and give them feedback on their performance no less than quarterly.

Ten Mistakes in Self-Management

Self-management is the key to being a successful manager. Think of the best managers you have worked for and emulate their techniques and strategies.

Let's review ten major mistakes that new managers make when managing themselves.

1. Being authoritarian.

Some managers become caught up in the power that comes with their new position and think their job is to be the final authority on everything. Avoid this trap. The greatest compliment you can give your employees or peers is to be willing to learn from them. As a manager, you do not need to know it all: you simply need to know whom to call on when you don't know something. If someone is willing to share their experience with you and offers to let you learn from their mistakes, take them up on that offer. Be coachable, and be willing to learn from your team, your peers, and your boss. No one expects you to know everything immediately, but they do expect you to be willing to ask for help when you need it and to be open to coaching along the way.

Your employees will not lose respect for you if they find out there's something that you don't know, but they will lose respect for you if you say you know something when you don't. They will respect you more when you are honest. Learn and grow by listening and observing others. Improve yourself by reading leadership books and articles, taking advantage of opportunities for training, accepting mentoring, and getting a coach.

2. Passivity.

The opposite of being too authoritarian is being passive: not knowing how to say no, not establishing boundaries, allowing others to dump on you. It is great to be helpful, but it is also OK to say, "No," "Not now," or "Not me." Don't take on additional work or try to solve a problem when you are not the appropriate person to do so. Although there are times when your expertise and knowledge will be needed, don't let yourself become the dumping zone for everyone else's problems and unwanted work. Be assertive: stand up for yourself without violating the rights of others. Passive people violate their own rights when they do not stand up for themselves. You can certainly give

> **Ten Mistakes in Self-Management**
> 1. Being authoritarian
> 2. Passivity
> 3. Avoiding difficult conversations
> 4. Not having fun
> 5. Not leaving personal problems at the door
> 6. Public criticism
> 7. Failing to prioritize people skills
> 8. Ignoring burnout
> 9. Ignoring stress
> 10. Failing to celebrate the wins

guidance, support, and direction to your employees, but they need to be able to depend on themselves, not always on you.

> Don't let yourself become the dumping zone for everyone else's problems.

3. Avoiding difficult conversations.

Learn how to approach the difficult conversations that every manager will eventually need to have regarding such issues as a negative performance review, personal hygiene, or a disciplinary action. There are good techniques that you can use to get through these types of conversations.

Let's consider a three-step feedback model you can implement that can be used in any or in many different scenarios.

Step 1 is to acknowledge the person and their emotions. You make them feel seen and heard. This is called *empathy*, and it is essential when having a difficult conversation. You can say something like, "I can see that you're frustrated," or "I'm sensing that you are upset."

Step 2 is to use "I" statements to communicate your concern to the person. Say, "I feel," "I overheard," "I noticed," "I'm concerned with," or "What I heard is . . ." or "What I observed is . . ." By using "I" statements, you are making an observation, unlike "you" statements, which come across as accusatory or blaming. These are likely to shut the other person down. Your goal is to keep them open. Avoid the use of absolutes and exaggerations, like "always" and "never."

Avoid saying "you" if at all possible, because it sets up defensive reactions. Speak for yourself: "I noticed this." "I observed that." "I was told this." "I need that." "I desire this." Always speak in behavioral terms. Don't attack the person. Attack the issue, whether it's a missed deadline, an issue of time and attendance, or inappropriate conduct. Whenever possible, avoid speaking about attitude: it's too vague to be of any help. Speak about the objective behaviors that you have observed that make you believe this person has a negative attitude. Speak to the behaviors; don't speak to the attitude. If you use "I" statements, stick to the facts, encourage input, and always respond with tact, you're going to be successful.

Step 3 is to invite feedback. Ask them to share their feedback or input to resolve the problem or concern. This keeps the mutuality of the conversation open. It allows them to contribute to the resolution.

4. Not having fun.
Work is serious business, so it helps to break up the monotony to have some fun once in a while. Use your judgment about the kinds of activities that would be appropriate for your workplace. But remember to have some fun.

5. Not leaving personal problems at the door.
Leaving your personal problems at the door is often easier said than done, but when you are at work, focus on the work. Sometimes doing so helps you get your mind off what is troubling you at home.

6. Public criticism.
Never give negative feedback in front of anyone else. Feedback should be given in private, not public. Give feedback in a calm way, without using raised voices or threatening body language. Many managers let their emotions get in their way and have raised their voice, yelled, or even berated an employee in public. This is embarrassing for both the employee and the manager, and the manager can lose credibility and trust.

7. Failing to prioritize people skills.
The more we rely on technology, the more valuable people skills become. We expect employees to interact with artificial intelligence and communicate over chat, instant messaging, and video calls instead of in person. Nonetheless, your people skills are essential to building trusting, respectful relationships with your employees and peers. Although

your technical skills may have gotten you to where you are today, your people skills will drive your future advancement. A good manager has good people skills. Don't undervalue them.

8. Ignoring burnout.

You are now responsible for yourself and your team, customers, and family. Do not ignore burnout. If you don't take care of yourself, you will not be able to take care of anyone else. For most of us, there is a never-ending mountain of work to be done. If you don't take care of yourself, you will not be around to do that work. Take frequent breaks throughout the day. Take your lunch break, and walk away when you're feeling burnout or overwhelmed. Find harmony between your work and your home life, which requires constant tuning and attention. Make this a daily goal and give both sides your best.

9. Ignoring stress.

There are techniques for managing stress, and every manager ought to learn them. You have a stressful job. Don't let the stressors get the best of you. You can manage and minimize stress in as little as one minute at a time. Set your timer for one minute and focus on your breathing. Let all the thoughts that are entering your mind pass by; acknowledge them and let them go. If you need help letting the thoughts go, focus on something else: count something, think back to your last vacation, or plan your next vacation. At the conclusion of the minute, notice how you feel. You can take short one-minute breaks throughout the day to manage your stress and reenergize yourself.

10. Failing to celebrate the wins.

If you are recognized for your team's accomplishments, share it with your team, and acknowledge their part in the success. When one of your employees gets a reward or your team accomplishes the company's goals, you are a big part of that success. Without your leadership and motivation, your team's accomplishments wouldn't have been possible, and it really is a great feeling. Never miss an opportunity to celebrate.

Key Points in This Chapter

In this chapter, we've covered five major themes:
1. Know your job.
2. Focus on the right things.
3. Know your team members.
4. Lead your team.
5. Manage yourself.

Consider setting one goal for each of these areas. Review your goals daily. Celebrate every win that you have in accomplishing your goals.

THREE

Building Teamwork

In this chapter, we're going to talk about building teamwork one individual at a time. We'll discuss the foundational aspects of teams as well as important factors to consider when putting a team together. We're also going to talk about individual team members and some things that might influence team dynamics. We will then go on to discuss vital dimensions that need to be considered when putting a team together, keeping it moving forward in unity, and reaching your goals and objectives. We'll also explore some key leadership practices.

Each leader will have to build a team as well as making corrections, providing feedback, and offering recognition and praise.

If possible, reflect on certain factors and take them into account before even putting the team together. If the team is already in place, it may need to be modified, and some members' roles may need to change. Moreover, there are temporary action teams as well as more permanent ones, so we'll talk about some of the key aspects of that topic too.

Choosing Team Members

When you're putting together a new team, you first have to determine how many people you need. Who is going to be selected, and how? Are you, as team leader, going to select them? Will somebody else be choosing them for you? As some members join the team, will they involved in selecting other members? Is the leadership role to be shared, or solitary? Will it move around in the team?

You need to make the same considerations with each role: will the roles be permanent; will the same person keep that same role for as long as they are on the team? Or will they share roles from time to time?

You'll also have to consider abilities. What skills and talents will be required? Will they be the same, or will they differ based on the roles? Finally, will this team be remote, hybrid, or on-site? That will have a major impact on the numbers and types of people that you assign to the team.

If you have an existing team, ask yourself, is it working? Is it optimum—where it needs it to be? If you do not start with a proper assessment, you will end up with a failed diagnosis. So the assessment of the unity level of that team is going to be critical going forward. Again, are the roles going to be shared? Are they going to be solitary? Will this change? Maybe right now they're solitary roles, but you may decide that you want to interchange roles among members. Will the current team members be able to absorb that? Will that work for them? Is that something that they are interested in doing or not? All of these things will have to be considered.

Further questions: do you need to add to or reduce the size of the team members based on workloads or capacity? Do you have suitable resources and tools? Are they contributing to team unity and success? If not, you perhaps need to do some research and get better, more efficient tools.

For an existing team, you certainly have to ask, what is your current success rate? If things are working really well, maybe you don't need to change anything, or very few things. If it's not, you need to find the root cause and determine if it's a matter of personal relations, resources, or leadership.

Temporary teams are very different from permanent teams. Will the specific task be single, or will it have to deal with several items? What is the projected lifespan of the team? Is it going to be short-term—just a few weeks—or do you expect it to last for a few months? Even a temporary team may last for a year or a year and a half.

How many people will you need? Are you going to add members as you go, and reevaluate? Research has shown that the smaller the team, the greater the likelihood of success. Larger numbers do not equate to more success. Typically, for an action team, four to six members is typical. If you have a permanent team with permanent roles, eight to twelve members is more likely. Anything larger than that can lead to dysfunction. The bigger the team, the greater the likelihood of dysfunction. If you end up with a team of over twelve to fifteen people, you might consider dividing it up into smaller subgroups.

> **The smaller the team, the greater the likelihood of success.**

You may have need of experts, but you might not want to incorporate them into the team permanently. There's nothing worse than sitting around at a meeting feeling as if you're not contributing or are wasting your time. You might be better served to invite experts and specialists in as needed and keep the decision-makers as a permanent part of the team.

With the temporary team, you'll have to consider how you are you going to keep them informed. Are you going to do that in bits and pieces? Are you going to do it abruptly, all at one time, at the conclusion? How is that going to work? That should be conveyed to the team in the beginning, if at all possible.

For permanent teams, you need to ask, how interdependent will the members be? Will they be doing a lot of individual work or a lot of interdependent work? That will partly determine the number of members. Will they be selected from within the company or outside the company? Who will make those selections? If at all possible, it's desirable to have team members involved in the hiring process, focusing on team fit as well as job fit.

As for the task itself, is the workload going to go up and down? Some people are very adaptive, with high flexibility levels. Some people are not. You can't teach flexibility: this is a quality that people have within them. Many of your decisions in this regard will be based on past experience. Have they been successful in those types of environments previously?

Finally, what tools and resources is the team currently using, and which ones do they need? If at all possible, involve the team members in this discussion. If you can wait until you form the team and then have them decide on the necessary tools, you'll be more successful, because they'll have agreed on these questions. Moreover, involvement equals commitment. Involving the team in decisions will make them feel they have a greater role, more responsibility, and more accountability.

Teams that have proven to be most successful are typically those whose members trust one another. Trust is built over time. The team leader might put together activities and make sure that the team's first couple of tasks are likely to be successful. This will build trust and respect among the team members who regularly work together, where they're face-to-face or online. Research has shown that most people work better in a face-to-face team environment.

In the most successful teams, members rely on one another to complete their tasks. When they're interdependent, they will of necessity have to form relationships. When people work independently, they don't rely on one another as much, so building relationships isn't as critical. In short, relationships will necessarily form more quickly in an interdependent group.

There is also the consideration of the environment: onsite, face-to-face, virtual, hybrid, or blended. Some people may work very well in a virtual environment; others may not. Research has shown that most people are more productive in a virtual environment, because there's less disruption. But numerous studies have also shown that some people are not cut out for this type of work.

Situational familiarity is another important consideration. If people have worked in, say, a blended or a virtual environment, it may be easier for them to do it again. That doesn't mean that somebody who's never worked in this context can't succeed, but you're going to have to look at their past experience and their preferences to determine how well they're suited to your particular choice of working environment. Their attitudes and behavioral styles, particularly their capacity for self-motivation, will have to be taken into consideration.

Styles and Skills

A good blend of behavioral styles is necessary for most teams. Whether you're working on-site, virtually, or in a hybrid format, you will need people from all styles to keep the team grounded. You'll need team members who are meticulous and attentive to detail in order to prevent mistakes. But you'll also need people who are very creative and think in terms of the big picture, so you can move the team forward.

In general, there are four basic behavioral styles. Some people are task-oriented; others are people-oriented. Some people are more fast-paced, whereas others are cautious.

People also differ in their communication preferences—passive, aggressive, or assertive—and those preferences will come into play. Passive people tend to communicate more indirectly; those who are more aggressive are more likely to be direct, face-to-face communicators. You will have to take these differences into account when setting up team communication norms.

What skill levels will be necessary for your team? If it is a virtual or hybrid team, some participants may need extra training to use the virtual tools. Again it's best, if at all possible, to involve the team members in as many of these decisions as possible.

Generational Differences

Generational differences make a huge difference in people's willingness to work together. This doesn't mean that everybody in a given generation is a certain way; it just means that the majority of those people have certain preferences. Although they can do things in ways that work against their preferences, their preferences will likely never go away.

> Generational differences make a huge difference in people's willingness to work together.

Generational representation can have a major and profound impact on team dynamics, including accountability, communication effectiveness, learning preferences, views, values, and other aspects of team dynamics.

Today we are in a 5G workforce. We have five generations currently engaged in work in the United States. Generation Z is the youngest: from teens to late twenties. Generation Y, late twenties to early forties; Generation X, forties to late fifties. Then we have the two generations that are ending their careers. The boomer generation consists of those who are in the late fifties to the mid-seventies. Finally, there is what some people call the silent or traditionalist generation, and they're in their mid-seventies to nineties.

Some organizations have all five generations currently working, but in others, only two or three generations are predominant. You're going to need to take these considerations into account, because these generations look at work, and teamwork in particular, differently.

Generation Z, the youngest generation, prefers to work alone.

Generation Z, the youngest generation, prefers to work alone. They do not necessarily enjoy engaging in teamwork or collaboration. With them, we are talking about team building one person at a time. With this generation, it would be safe to assume that you should start them out in smaller teams. You may even want to start them out partnering with just one other team member and building that relationship over time.

Generation Y tends to regard teamwork as a natural environment. They understand that they need to work in a team in order to accomplish their tasks on time and with success. They're more than willing to collaborate with each other if they understand that the team environment and interrelationship are going to be necessary for work completion.

Generation X actually enjoys teamwork. You might even say they prefer teamwork, and they have a lot of success engaging in these collaborative tasks. At this particular time, this generation is typically in leadership positions. Since they tend to want to work in a team environment and the younger generation does not so much, that may create areas for conflict or confrontation.

Several studies have made it plain that millennials and Generation Y generally prefer collaboration. Generation Z does not: a study from 2017 found that 95 percent of Generation Z people desire an individual over a group approach. Two thirds of respondents said they preferred to have collaborations (if any) with small teams. This is why they prefer to work in offices and not cubicles. Some companies are going back to offices, because Gen Z prefers that type of work.

Boomers and traditionalists in the workforce are committed to teamwork and collaboration, but they want to see success in the effort. Otherwise, they become disenfranchised. With these employees, make sure to point out the team's successes.

The generations also have different outlooks on learning approaches. A majority of Xers and Yers prefer to learn both hard skills and soft skills on the job, whereas boomers and the silent generation prefer to learn soft skills on the job but want to learn technical skills in a classroom, with a formal setting. Young workers want just the opposite: they want to learn as they go, working hands-on.

As for leadership attributes, never assume that every person looks for the same thing in a leader. Generational attitudes come into play here as well. Older workers tend to look for credibility. They want to know that you know what you're talking about. They want to know that you have good judgment and make good decisions. Although trustworthiness is a critical factor for any leader, it is especially important for older workers. If they don't trust you, they're not going to follow you. You have to build trustworthiness in their eyes, and you can only do that through deeds.

Furthermore, the older generations want leaders who are farsighted. They want somebody who can plan for the long term, because they tend to want to stay in companies longer. From their point of view, it's going to be very important to plan not only for the month or the quarter, but maybe for the next five years. Even better if you can communicate that vision to the team or involve them in creating it.

Generation Xers also want somebody who they find credible, who has knowledge, and not just about the technical aspects of the work. Of course, no leader is going to be an expert in everything that every team member is doing, but certainly Gen Xers want to know that you have earned credibility from the team. This credibility includes leadership, knowing how to form teams, knowing how to coach and counsel, and even to discipline employees in the right way. They also highly value trust: to work with you, they have to trust you. This generation doesn't say, "I work for you"; they always look at it as "I work with you."

Dedication is another important quality for the younger generations. This is not just a matter of being dedicated to the company or getting the job done. They want to know that you're dedicated to them and their personal development, developing their skills and talents and providing training and opportunities for advancement and promotion.

The two younger generations—people from their teens to the early forties—want a leader who listens, because they expect to be able to provide input. They also want to know *why*. They will ask, why are we doing this? The team leader of today thus has to be ready to listen to questions and provide feedback.

These generations want to know that the leader is dependable. This is not just a matter of coming to work on time, but being somebody they can go to and ask when they run into obstacles. They also want somebody that they can depend on not to mislead them. This quality, again, is tied to trust. They have to know that they can trust us to provide the correct answers and the right information.

In terms of receptivity to feedback, while young workers prefer regular feedback, older workers such as boomers may be offended by it. Although you will have to gauge each person individually, in general you need to understand that older workers want less feedback, and younger workers want more.

In this context, always gauge yourself. Even in the most complex situation, where people desire a lot of feedback, you could provide too much, which they might see as micromanaging. Older workers in particular tend to view constant feedback as micromanaging, so you want to avoid this mistake especially with them.

Nonetheless, numerous research studies over the past five decades have shown that companies providing regular feedback outperform those without regular feedback systems. The most successful companies provide feedback, often every six weeks or twelve weeks, or semiannually. Research over the years has shown that annual evaluations and appraisals are not very effective.

It's also best to use an objective evaluation or feedback system, whereby you're focusing on objective behaviors or outcomes. Many companies use key performance indicators (KpIs) or MBO (management by objective) programs, which tend to be more successful.

Any type of feedback, whether positive or negative, should create a path forward. Don't wait; do it immediately. Make sure to provide feedback right away, in the least possible time after the activity in question, which will help workers understand better.

> **Any type of feedback, whether positive or negative, should create a path forward.**

Feedback also has to be accurate. The truth is all that matters, even when it's hard to swallow. Never sugarcoat your feedback, and certainly never exaggerate the situation and make it seem worse than it is. Just be accurate.

You want to be thorough and meticulous in this arena. Vague feedback will result in repeat mistakes. Be as specific as possible with your feedback, whether it's positive or negative. Say somebody carries out a task really well and there were three parts to the process. The employee did all three well, but did part two exceptionally well. Point that out to them, and be specific about exactly what you thought went exceptionally well for that particular part of the task.

The same is true with giving negative feedback. Let's say that two out of the three parts went well. Tell the employee that you thought those two came off successfully, but phase three had certain specific issues. Then ask them what they would do differently next time.

All feedback must foster positive outcomes. Even if you're delivering negative feedback, you have to do it in a way that will lead to a positive outcome the next time.

An old saying, which is still true today, says that telling is not leading. When at all possible, allow the employee to come up with their own solutions. If they can't come up with any, of course you have to offer our own.

Telling is not leading.

Although you may have to offer multiple options, you don't necessarily want to tell the employee what to do; you want to offer them suggestions that they can choose from. You might use a leading statement like, "Bob, have you thought about this?" or "Nancy, have you considered that?" When you put it that way, they can think about it and say, "I'd never thought about it. If I did it that way, I would probably be more successful or more comfortable with the job." Then you simply ask, "Is that the way you're going to choose to do it next time?" When they say, "Yes, that's the way I'm going to do it," it was their choice, not yours. If you tell somebody to do something a certain way and it doesn't work, they can blame you. But if they choose to do something a certain way (even if they're following a suggestion from you), they chose to do it, so they don't get to blame you; they can only blame themselves. There's a higher level of accountability with this method than in simply telling them what to do.

Finally, you have to be receptive to feedback and criticism, because if you're going to give it, you have to be able to take it.

The Unity Process

These considerations bring us to the unity process. It consists of several dimensions, all of which will be needed in order to form the team, keep it together, and keep it focused on its goals and objectives.

When you put together a team, you need to make sure that you set norms and expectations to lead the team to desired behaviors. These norms are typically developed through regular interactions among team members, including role modeling from team leaders. But it's preferable in the beginning to sit down with the team and develop written norms for matters like holding meetings (especially if you're going to have virtual meetings). You may need to decide how you will talk to people. Will you accept members' opinions for what they are: their opinions? Will you look at the positive and negative aspects of what people put forward?

Everybody needs to agree to these norms, so they become the expectation. Once you set them, the process is typically palatable for the team members. They accept the fact that this is how this particular team is operating, and most people will operate within them. Another advantage is that it's easier to hold team members accountable and call them out when they don't abide by the norms.

Once you've agreed upon these norms, put them in writing, and make sure everybody gets a copy of it. You might need to review and renegotiate them from time to time. You may have to raise or lower your standard depending on your progress. In any event, you want to put these standards in place right up front, because they will ensure that every activity within the team accords with the norms.

Creating team unity involves creating ownership. Team members must understand the costs and measure progress; everybody should understand the expected results as well as the benefits. What will be the benefits to the company, the team, the individual members, and the clients and customers?

How do you create team ownership? Ownership equals commitment. If you own something, you're going to be more committed to it. To make sure the team members are committed, involve them in setting the goals and objectives. This will prevent pushback and resistance and cut down on the implementation time.

Say you as team leader go into your office and create three to five critical objectives for the next quarter and deliver those objectives to the team. They may sit there and look at you and agree with every one of them while you're there talking with them. You might not get much feedback at all. They may truly think that this is the right way to go, but they could just as easily think that you are headed in the wrong direction. They could believe that some of these objectives aren't necessary. They also might think that some of the goals are too unrealistic or are set too low. Involving the team in goal setting works all these issues out in the beginning and incorporates everybody's voice.

To be effective, the team will have to have shared communication about every aspect of the work. After all, they're interdependent, and that means that goals should be interdependent.

There has to be a personal commitment to these objectives: each and every member has to be personally committed to their role in attaining them. The only way to do that is to make sure they understand and to ask them for commitment. Say, "Do you understand your role in the team's accomplishing its goals? What can we do to make sure that your particular jobs or tasks will be accomplished? Do you see any obstacles?" Commit to helping them, and then ask them to commit to you. They will bring any obstacles to your attention or that of the other team members.

Next, make sure you have regular follow-up, perhaps once a week in most situations. Some managers try to follow up every day, but you have to be careful here, because you don't want to come across as a micromanager. If at all possible, use software to keep track of this process. People can check in or use a communication mechanism to provide ongoing check-ins.

You also want to give team members credit for helping establish these goals and objectives as well as obtaining them.

How do you ensure that the team understands the costs? People have to understand what good work and bad work look like. Look at the different possible outcomes, and put on exact cost factors. How much will reworking a product or service actually cost the organization? What will the cost be if one or several individuals in the team have to go back and rework a particular aspect of the project? How will it bog the team down?

How do you measure progress? What tools are you going to use? Many organizations use key performance indicators (KPIs). Some organizations use matrices. Others simply use ongoing informal feedback on a daily or weekly basis. Typically, you need multiple methods of providing feedback and progress reports.

How frequently will you do this? What's right for your team?

Feedback should measure both the team's and the individuals' performance. You'll discuss individual performance one-on-one, whereas the team's performance is going to be measured as a whole.

When possible, let the team members have input on which measurements and tools will be used and how they will be used.

About thirty years ago, one gentleman who was running a shop would go out and give each and every worker their score. Every day he would write their efficiency score on a piece of paper. Simply because of this process, the performance of that work unit nearly doubled over just a few weeks' time. Employees had never had that before. People want to know where they stand.

This employer also knew that peer pressure enhances performance. Later, he would provide employees with recognition if they scored at a certain level, which boosted performance even more. But simply handing them a score was enough to cause improvement. Today we refer to this as a *scorecard system*.

Peer pressure enhances performance.

How should you clarify expected results? It's preferable to do it in writing. The expectations should be written down. They have to be realistic. The team should also agree to them. Some managers have found that if they let team members set the expectations, the team typically sets them higher than the manager would. You'll even probably have to rein them in. Some of their expectations may be too lofty, and you certainly don't want to set a team up with unrealistic expectations, but give them some leeway.

The worst thing that can happen is setting expectations at an unrealistic level: then people will take on a defeatist attitude immediately and give up before they start.

The business world is no different from any other part of life: there will be obstacles, many of which are foreseeable. Plan for foreseeable obstacles. Make a list of the ones that you may encounter along the way and put together a plan for dealing with them. This will make the team respond better if these eventualities come about. It's a good idea to plan for the worst and hope for the best.

There are always chances for change. Talking about this fact in the beginning will make it easier for people to adapt when it does happen. Flexibility in the face of change is key. All team members need to accept the fact that this is business, and over time, business expectations change, perhaps because the company has to go in a different direction. Some new product may come out that affects your own product line.

Finally, how should you go about identifying the observable benefits? Here's one tip. After you and your team create the goals and objectives and have them written out, get the team together and ask, "How is it going to benefit the organization when we reach these goals?" Ask how these accomplishments will benefit the organization, the shareholders, and the employees individually. Very likely they'll come up with all kinds of potential benefits.

Over the years, a number of very successful team leaders have simply asked individuals for their personal goals and objectives. Team members are asked what benefits they would like to see from the work and how they can be incorporated into the larger objectives and the benefits for the team itself. If people can see the connection, they're more likely to work harder.

Key Leadership Practices

Key leadership practices are essential. These are things you *have* to do. Otherwise, the team is likely going to be derailed.

There's no such thing as a perfect environment. Some employees will have very high work standards and ethics. Others will struggle. Some employees will be great at working in a team environment; others, not. Some employees are great communicators; others, not so much. The team leader will have to take these individual differences into account.

Here are some practices and approaches that have been proven to work.

To be effective, leadership has to result in earned authority acquired over time. People will not follow you simply because you've been assigned to a job. They will follow you as a role model; if not, they will find somebody to serve as their leader.

In short, you will have to work hard to earn three things from your subordinates: they will have to trust you, they will have to respect you, and they will have to find you credible. Without these qualities, there is no way that they're going to allow you to lead or inspire them in any meaningful sense.

Associates will follow you, listen to you, and work harder if they trust you. But in order to earn their trust, you have to trust them first. This is why micromanagers have such a hard time: they demonstrate every single day that they don't trust people. Therefore, employees aren't inspired by them. They'll do what they're asked, but they typically don't do any more. They'll do the minimum. The problem with micromanagers is they have low trust in themselves, which is why they have low trust in other people. As a manager, you have to let go. You have to be able to step away and allow your staff to act and make mistakes. Until they prove that they *can't* do a certain task, you have to empower them. This will let them show exactly how much they can do.

If you allow your associates to learn from their mistakes, they're going to look at work as a learning opportunity. Encourage self-reflection, especially when coaching and counseling people. Let them tell you what they think went well and what they think didn't. Allow them to solve their own problems and then ask them for a commitment based on their solution. Say, "What I hear you saying is, you're going to do this and this the next time this happens, and you think you'll have a different outcome." They may say, "Yeah, I'm going to do that." Then you can turn around and affirm your belief in their abilities: "I think if you do those two things, you are going to be successful. I know that you've done even more challenging things in the past, and I think it's going to work out for you in the long run."

Successful leaders also have to keep their promises. If you promise somebody something and you have to break that promise, you need to explain why. Don't push the blame off on somebody else; take ownership. Of course, there may be factors beyond your control, but it's best to never shift blame, even onto the organization. Step up and say, "I told you I could do this, and I didn't. In this case, I thought I had control, but I didn't. I'm taking total responsibility. In the future, I won't make promises that I don't have total control over." Coming clean with associates will create a higher level of respect and trust.

Moreover, you have to stand up for your associates. One of the main keys to success is when the team does really well, the leader will stand up in front of the rest of the company and say, "This person pulled together and made it happen."

On the other hand, when the team doesn't reach its objectives, the leader has to stand up in front of the company and say, "It's my fault. I didn't train them right. I didn't give them the right focus. I didn't give them the tools and the resources necessary."

You have to be willing to stand up for your subordinates in the moment of truth. If you're unwilling to do that, you will never earn their trust.

Stand up for your subordinates.

It's also vital to admit your mistakes. Over and over again, surveys by human resource organizations indicate that employees always place this quality in the top few attributes of good leaders.

Employees like leaders who will admit their mistakes. It makes them feel that workers could admit their own mistakes without fear of being attacked or belittled. After all, good judgment comes from bad judgment. Behavior experts tell us that we learn more from our mistakes than we do our successes. In any event, mistakes are going to happen. The important thing is how we deal with them. Do we use them as learning opportunities, or do we use them to demean or belittle someone? Belittling will only hurt or break the relationship.

Sometimes you might need to challenge somebody with a task that you know they're not going to be comfortable with. You can tell them, "I want you to do this because I think you're going to be good at it." Hopefully that's a truthful statement. Certainly you don't want to mislead or lie to them. But assign them a new task if you think they will be good at it, even if they haven't done it before and even if it causes some discomfort. Make sure to support them, or assign a buddy who can. Adding new duties will broaden and stretch that associate and perhaps even open up new opportunities for them.

Your subordinates have to respect you, so you're always going to have to set an example. Be early and stay late if necessary. Chip in when your staff needs you. Act ethically. Nothing is worse than working in a team where the team leader is unethical, where they steal, where they lie, and where they encourage other people to do those things. When you set the example of that kind of behavior, others will certainly follow.

Cutting corners in the work can also be unethical. Do you cut corners to meet the deadline? Or do you say, "OK, we're not going to meet the deadline, but we're going to put out a safe and high-quality product"? These things matter in the eyes of associates, because in every moment of every day, you are teaching them how to work. Of course you need to set realistic goals, but if they're challenging as well, employees will work harder.

The final characteristic a supervisor needs is credibility. Double-check your work. Everybody makes mistakes, but you need to make as few as you can. Don't shoot from the hip. If you don't know the answer, just simply say, "I don't have all the facts right now. If you have some input, I'd like to hear from you and make that decision later." Again, you always want to ask for staff input. Successful leaders know when to ask the questions and whom to ask. They get as much input as they can from those experts and make a decision based on the input.

You need to study and research to make sure you're prepared. But you don't want to be a know-it-all. You might want to ask for input, even if you know the answer. In that case, you can simply say, "Hey, you know what? I agree with

John." This will elevate the employee. Their self-esteem and credibility among their team members will go up, and you'll have a happier and better team. It's not necessary to know all the answers; as a matter of fact, you probably won't. By welcoming staff input and doing your research, you'll know that the suggestions they make are the right ones.

Effective coaches educate. Teaching and inspiring are the core tasks of any coach. You have to provide the means, tools, and resources to do the job. You have to provide focus and objectives (and remember, you need to do that jointly with associates). You have to offer support and understanding. Some employees will struggle with certain tasks, and certain projects, even though they're exceptional in other areas. Everybody has talents. You may have put them in a losing role: not everybody can do every job. You have to be able to assess their strengths, abilities, and weaknesses and place them in the right situation to win.

Effective coaches educate.

From time to time, you will have employees who have issues outside the workplace. If they have a personal or family emergency, put the work aside and focus on that employee. Make sure to focus on helping them through their issue, because at this point they're not going to be effective at work anyway. Don't make the mistake of damaging the relationship because you didn't focus on their true needs in favor of the work.

One important quality of effective leaders is that they focus on the positive instead of the negative. As a supervisor, you may have to deliver bad news, but you don't have to attach a judgment to it.

One supervisor didn't understand this fact. At the morning meeting, if he had five things to tell the staff, he always brought up the worst thing first, and before he said it, he would tell them it was going to be bad. He would introduce the topic with a statement like this: "You're not going to believe what they're asking us to do," or "You're not going to like this." No matter what came out of his mouth next, it meant that the staff wasn't supposed to like it. Sometimes the staff would even say, "Oh, that's not that bad. We can fix this."

This manager never was self-aware enough to know the negative impact that he was having. For people who already had negative tendencies, it was like putting fuel on the fire. You'd have a big bonfire of negativity.

Conversely, don't put a positive spin on a negative announcement. Just deliver the news. Let the staff make their own assessments. If you want to get them out of a pool of negativity, focus on solutions and outcomes. Tell them, "I'm sure we can reach a better solution. We have a ton of knowledge and a ton of dedication here. If we put our heads together, we can solve this problem."

When people are dealing with change (as they almost certainly have to do), they're typically going to be somewhat resistant. Help them to see that the changes are not going to affect them in a negative way, or may even affect them in a positive way (if that is the case).

Understand also that change is individual. Some people can accommodate it better than others. Some focus on the past; others focus on the future. Use that to your advantage.

People who focus on the past are typically trying to prevent mistakes. Play to that strength: in one-on-one settings (that is, before you get into a team environment), you may want to discuss the things they see as potential obstacles or causes of conflict and confrontation. If people are focused on the future and on possibilities, encourage that behavior too, although at times you might have to rein in the enthusiasm.

Accountability

Accountability is extremely important, because it is tied up with motivation and performance. Without accountability, employees will not be able to justify or explain their actions. Supervisors need to develop guidelines and standards for conduct, evaluate individual performance using those standards, and give rewards or disciplines based on that assessment.

We've already discussed expectations, outcomes, coaching, and regular check-ins. Provide ongoing training; assess your staff's strengths and weaknesses. Make sure you've got adequate on-the-job training for those who desire it. Make sure you blend in technical training for those who want it.

Acknowledge the other person; acknowledge their situation; acknowledge their emotions, if they're emotional; use "I" statements; state facts and invite feedback. If you practice doing these things, you're likely to be very successful in holding people accountable.

Key Points in This Chapter

The main theme of this chapter is building teams and what this requires from you as a supervisor, from the individuals involved, and for the team as a whole. The chapter explored team dynamics and how to keep it moving forward toward its objectives. It also outlined some key leadership practices.

FOUR

Unlocking Your Executive Presence

One statistic says that about 26 percent of what it takes to get promoted to leadership roles is a quality called *executive presence*. Yet for many of us, executive presence feels like a vague, hard to pin down concept. What is it? More importantly, how do you develop it?

These questions are the ones that this chapter will attempt to address. It will break down this somewhat mysterious concept of executive presence and talk about practical ways you can develop your own executive presence. It will discuss how to communicate more effectively and how to present yourself with confidence in order to navigate the tricky waters of office politics. Ideally, this chapter will enable you to have a solid game plan for developing that crucial 26 percent of your leadership potential.

This chapter is divided into five major parts. In part 1, we'll consider the foundations of executive presence. Part 2 will discuss mastering communication and influence. Part 3 is about professional image and networking. In part 4, we'll talk about pitfalls to avoid and how to cultivate success. And in part 5, we'll explore continual growth and self-investment.

Foundations of Executive Presence

Let's start by understanding what executive presence is and how it can affect career growth. Executive presence is a nuanced concept, often mistaken for general leadership qualities. To understand it, we must consider how executives are selected. While education, experience, and professional networks are very important, companies seek additional qualities in their senior leaders; a specific X factor that transcends conventional metrics. This somewhat elusive attribute is known as *executive presence*. Unlike tangible qualifications, executive presence isn't easily defined or measured. It's a combination of traits and behaviors that distinguish exceptional leaders. These qualities go beyond standard leadership skills, encompassing how individuals carry themselves and communicate and influence others around them in high-stakes professional environments.

Understanding executive presence involves seeing its subtle yet powerful impact on leadership effectiveness and career advancement. These qualities can set apart equally qualified candidates in executive hiring decisions. Our discussion will help you see how you can fully develop your executive presence.

Sylvia Ann Hewlett, an economist and author, identifies three pillars of executive presence. The first pillar that she mentions is *gravitas*: the weight of your personality and the confidence that you project. It's evident when people take

> **Three Pillars of Executive Presence**
> 1. Gravitas
> 2. Communication skills
> 3. Appearance

you seriously, value your opinion, and hesitate to question your statements or decisions. Gravitas isn't innate: it's a skill that can be developed over time. Don't worry if you don't think you possess this capacity right now. You can work on honing and crafting the weight that you carry into business situations.

Hewlett's next pillar is *communication skills.* In the context of executive presence, effective communication means speaking confidently and concisely, supporting your statements with data, and convincing others of your ideas. It also involves inspiring your team and setting achievable goals. While exceptional eloquence is beneficial, it's not essential for strong executive presence.

The third pillar is *appearance*: not your physical attractiveness or personality, but how you present yourself professionally. It involves understanding and adhering to unwritten workplace norms, dressing appropriately for your environment, and carrying yourself with confidence. The key here is to adapt your appearance to suit different workplace cultures and situations.

These three elements combined contribute to a strong executive presence, which can and will significantly impact your professional effectiveness and, in many cases, your career progress. Developing a strong executive presence can open doors to leadership positions and career advancement opportunities. It's increasingly seen as a key requirement for leadership roles. Leaders with excellent executive presence have an aura of personal power combined with a generous and engaging communication style that allows them to be more influential, solution-focused, inspiring, and motivational.

To cultivate executive presence, it's crucial to actively shape how others perceive you. This involves a combination of consistent behaviors, interpersonal skills, and personal development. It's not about manipulation or being someone that you're not.

Key Strategies for Executive Presence

Let's look at some key strategies that you can employ to influence other people's perceptions of you.

The first one is to be consistent in your behavior and communication. Maintain a steady demeanor across various situations. Align your words with your actions in order to build trust and develop a reliable communication style that others can depend on. Be consistent in your behavior and communication style. Be the same person every time people see you.

Practice active listening, and show genuine interest in others. You want to give full attention to the person that you're speaking with. Show them that you're listening by asking thoughtful follow-up questions and demonstrating empathy and understanding. Even if you don't fully feel what the other person is feeling in the moment, think about it, and do your best to put yourself in their shoes and show you are trying to understand them. Trying to understand someone, even when you don't agree with their point of view, is an aspect of executive presence on which many don't work hard enough (much less master), but it is key. Remember and refer to details from past interactions. That will be very important, because people will know that you listened, you cared, and you remembered.

Develop a strong personal brand.

Next, develop a strong personal brand. Identify your unique strengths and values. Make a list. What are my strengths? What are my weaknesses? What do I hold dear? What are my values? What are my ethics? What are my morals? Use that outline to craft a clear professional narrative, bringing who you are in your personal life into who you are in your professional life.

Again, be the same person every time people see you, whether it's face-to-face, on camera, or on social media. Be sure that your online presence aligns with your in-person persona.

Network strategically to reinforce your brand. Meet up with other like-minded people. Share your thoughts, opinions, and experiences in your network, and reinforce the brand that you are bringing to the organization or to any situation that you find yourself in.

When you meet challenges, cultivate a positive attitude and approach. Think about framing obstacles as growth opportunities. Maintain your composure when you're under pressure. Be in control of your emotions. Be tactful. Don't be quick to snipe or snark. Inspire confidence in others through your optimism. When a challenge arises or some unpopular change is coming, don't roll your eyes with everyone else, being negative and pessimistic. Focus on the good; focus on the solution. By doing so, you'll lead by example in tough situations that require an executive level of problem-solving skills.

Continually work on improving your skills and your knowledge. Stay updated on industry trends and best practices. Seek feedback and act on it constructively. Invest in professional development and learning opportunities, and share your expertise generously with colleagues. Avoid becoming a know-it-all, but be a helpful source of information (admittedly, there is a fine line between the two).

Master nonverbal communication. Develop strong eye contact and open posture when you're speaking with people. Use confident body language and gestures. If you're hunched over or your head is down, it may send the wrong message. Be confident, be up, be open, chin up.

Pay attention to your tone of voice and your speaking pace.

You could, for example, say, "I like that sweater." Depending upon the tone and inflection of your voice, it could convey either sarcasm or a kind of sinister overenthusiasm. You could go from confident to creepy in a matter of seconds.

Think about how your voice sounds to others. Record yourself. (That's no big problem: we can do that on our phones today.) Pay attention to how quickly or slowly you speak. If you're talking too fast, you'll lose people. You might start to sound like white noise to them. But if you talk too slow, you could find that they're waiting for you to shut up; they don't even hear anything you're saying, because they're bored. Find yourself somewhere in the middle in terms of tone, pace, pitch, and volume, and you will definitely be able to manage verbal and nonverbal cues along the way.

Build and leverage connections with colleagues at all levels. Offer support and mentorship to others. Collaborate effectively across departments and teams, showing that you're the kind of person who knows how to work with others instead of always having to be the boss. The best leaders are also the best followers. Show yourself to be someone who could step into either role and have appreciation for both.

Display emotional intelligence.

Much of what was said above boils down to this: Display emotional intelligence: this will inspire others to see you as a role model for their own executive presence. Manage your emotions effectively. Read and respond appropriately to others' emotional cues, and navigate complex interpersonal dynamics with tact. If you find it difficult to read cues and navigate the dynamics of interpersonal relationships, don't be afraid to share that with people in your network so they won't misperceive your responses as something negative.

Above all, remember that executive presence is *not* pretending to be someone you are not. It's about bringing the best version of yourself and projecting it confidently in professional settings. Authenticity is key. Amplify and refine your natural strengths rather than adopting an artificial persona. Be authentic: this will be appreciated and will only improve the way other people see you.

Mastering Communication and Influence

Effective communication is at the heart of executive presence. As we've seen, it's not just about what you say, but how you say it and how well you listen to others.

Let's look at communication and influence skills that a person must possess and master to have a strong executive presence.

Effective communication across all mediums is crucial for developing executive presence.

First, think about in-person communication. Remember the basics here. Maintain eye contact: it shows you're engaged and confident. Use appropriate gestures to emphasize your points, but don't go overboard. You're not conducting an orchestra. Speak with clarity and confidence, even if you're nervous. Do your best to put yourself in a confident mindset and bring your best self to the conversation. When thinking about virtual communication, this is more important than ever.

For webinars or video calls, good lighting is key. Nobody wants to feel as if they're talking to a shadow puppet, so bring the lights up a little bit. Make sure your background looks professional (no piles of laundry behind you). And here's a tip: when talking directly to individuals on camera, look into the camera. It might feel weird, but it creates a sense of connection, which is going to be very important for personal conversations.

Don't forget about written communication. In your emails, reports, and other written materials, be clear, concise, and professional. Your written words represent you when you're not there to represent yourself in person.

Now let's talk about articulating a vision that aligns with organizational goals. This is how you really start to influence others and show leadership potential.

Clearly communicate your ideas, but here's the kicker: show how they align with the company's objectives. This demonstrates that you're thinking about the big picture. Use storytelling techniques: people remember stories better than dry facts. Make your vision relatable and memorable by wrapping it in a compelling narrative. Finally, back it up with concrete examples and data, but when you incorporate your facts into your stories, you'll have a better response. Especially to other executives, numbers talk, but stories engage. Stories make you relatable, but you will always have to provide solid evidence to support your points you're making. Executive presence isn't just about what you say: it's about how you say it, how you present it, and how you get others to buy into your vision.

Active Listening

Let's talk a little bit more about active listening skills, which are crucial for engaging with others. You definitely want to give others your full attention, because that is what you want from them. It goes both ways: you model the behavior that you want to receive. Moreover, giving your full attention to the speaker will enable you to gain their trust and respect.

> **Active listening skills are crucial for engaging with others.**

As the other person is talking, ask clarifying questions at appropriate intervals. Again, it shows that you're listening and interested. You're not just sitting there; you're really engaged with them. Paraphrase what they've said back to them to make sure that you've understood what they said and what they meant by it.

Provide thoughtful feedback. Tell the other person what you appreciate about what they said. If there's something that you're not clear about or disagree with, think before you give feedback. Engage with the other person in a way that shows that you care. You're not there to criticize; you're there to converse and listen.

You want to inspire confidence across all levels, so you want to be well prepared for meetings and presentations. Be prepared for the meeting. If you are the presenter, be ready to give the supporting information. Speak with authority and conviction. Use your demeanor and the passion with which you speak to show that you know what you're talking about and you are someone to be taken seriously.

Don't be a know-it-all. Be open to feedback and ideas from others. You may not be giving your presentation in a way that someone understands or appreciates. Maybe they're bold enough to tell you that during the meeting. You may not always agree with what they say, but be open to receiving it, hearing it, and thanking someone for their feedback, even when you don't agree. It's never a bad thing to hear what someone is thinking, rather than having them bottle up their thoughts so that you never really know how they felt about the information you delivered.

Finally, acknowledge and celebrate team success. It's not all about me; it's about us and our team. As the team leader, you're going to get a lot of the credit, but don't be a credit hog. Draw the whole team into the conversation. Make sure to say, "I couldn't have done it without them." That will buy you more respect as well as enhancing your gravitas.

Many if not most of us operate under stress more frequently than we would like. When you're doing so, maintain composure, practice mindfulness, and employ stress management, like deep breathing and meditation.

Preparation is key to managing stress in high-pressure situations. If you are thoroughly prepared, you will handle them more effectively. Stay focused on solutions rather than problems. If someone brings you a problem, focus on the workable solution instead of just digging deeper into the problem. Maintain a positive attitude. Even in the most challenging of circumstances, showing positivity through your demeanor and body language will help you grow and improve your executive presence.

By mastering these skills, you'll be well on your way to developing a strong presence that commands respect and attention in virtually any professional setting.

Professional Image and Networking

Your professional image and network play crucial roles in establishing and maintaining executive presence. They contribute significantly to how others perceive you and can open doors to new opportunities and adventures.

Let's start with making sure your appearance reflects your confidence. It matters more than you might think. We always hear people say, "Dress for success," but do we really know what that means?

This will depend on your industry and your role within the organization. A suit might be perfect in a law firm, but it could look out of place in a tech startup. The key is to dress appropriately for the context.

Don't forget the little things. Grooming details matter. A well-pressed shirt, a neat hairstyle, and a neatly trimmed beard can make a world of difference. Here's another tip: choose clothing that makes you feel like a million dollars. When you feel confident and comfortable, it will show through. Your appearance should match the image that you want to project. Think about how you want others to perceive you and dress accordingly.

Body language is a key component of your image. It's not what you say, but how you say it—and how you look while you're saying it. Good posture instantly makes you look more confident. Make eye contact, but don't stare: that could be off-putting. Use gestures to emphasize your points, but keep them controlled and purposeful. Pay careful attention to your facial expressions. They can give away more than you intend and often send a message that you had no idea you were transmitting.

Networking

A solid professional network can seriously boost your executive presence. Attend industry events and conferences. Join professional associations, and don't neglect social media. LinkedIn isn't just for job hunting: it's a powerful networking tool, and there are many similar websites out there.

Here's the real secret: offer to help and support others within your network. People remember those who have helped them. Be a memorable person in that context.

> Offer to help and support others within your network.

Organizational politics: nobody likes it (or they say they don't), but being politically savvy is crucial for executive presence. You need to be able to understand the formal and informal power structures in your organization. Build good, positive relationships with key stakeholders. Always be diplomatic in your interactions. You never know who might be your ally or your opponent in the near future. Stay in the loop. Stay informed about organizational changes and priorities. Know what's happening in your organization, because you may ultimately want to be in a role where you effect substantial change in that organization.

Driving change is one area where you can shine and build your executive presence. Start by clearly explaining why a change is needed. Get people on board. Let them be on your side. Build a coalition of supporters. Develop a clear implementation plan. Have a solid plan for how the change is going to work and hopefully head off any bumps in the road, or address them as they occur.

Communicate progress and celebrate successes. Keep everyone updated on the progress of the initiative of the change, and make sure to give the people who deserve it the congratulations and celebration that they have earned.

When you focus on all these aspects—your appearance, your body language, network, political savvy, and leadership in change leadership—you will be well on your way to perfecting your executive presence. It's all about projecting confidence, competence, and ultimately leadership.

The Dos and Don'ts of Executive Presence

Developing executive presence is as much about what to avoid as what to do. Understanding common pitfalls and how to overcome them can help you cultivate a strong and authentic presence in your organization.

Think about this as a list of the dos and the don'ts of cultivating executive presence. Let's start with the dos.

1. **Embrace authenticity.** People can spot a fake a mile away. This is about bringing your best, most authentic self to every interaction.
2. **Continual learning and self-improvement.** Keep learning, keep improving. The moment you think you know

it all is the moment you start falling behind and losing respect.
3. **Welcome constructive feedback** from peers and mentors. Even when it's tough to hear, listen to it, and look for opportunities to step outside of your comfort zone. As a matter of fact, don't just look at them, seize them. It may be difficult at first, but it is a necessity for developing executive presence.

Now that you know what to embrace, what do you want to avoid?
1. **Ditch the arrogance.** Confidence is great, but nobody likes a know-it-all.
2. **Inconsistency in your behavior and communication.** Flip-flopping is not a quality that people love. They want you to be reliable, and if you do not appear to be reliable, they will question you.
3. **Don't neglect relationships.** They are the oil that keeps the corporate engine running. You want to have good relationships with colleagues, coworkers, clients, the community—whatever that looks like in your organization. Don't neglect your important relationships.
4. **Resist the urge to resist change.** Adaptability is key in today's fast-paced world. Just because you don't like a change doesn't mean it's not a good thing. Model positive behavior, so that when you are effecting change in your organization and getting pushback, you will be able to speak as someone who has not resisted change but embraced it.

Avoiding Common Mistakes

Now let's talk about some common mistakes that you can make when crafting and improving your executive presence, and how to avoid them.

1. **Focusing too much on self-promotion.** Of necessity, crafting your executive presence comes with an element of self-promotion. But if that's all you do, it will cause people to tune you out and turn away. What's the solution? Balance self-promotion with genuine interest in others and their contributions. It will come back to you many times over.

2. **Neglecting to adapt your communication style.** As we've already seen, there is no such thing as a one-size-fits-all communicator. Different people have different communication styles and preferences. Practice flexibility in your approach to communication, and base it on the needs of your audience. What works for your team might not work in the boardroom or with a client, so be adaptable.

    Sometimes you don't know what you're walking into: an uncertain situation, a stressful situation, or a joyful one. Think of yourself as a sort of chameleon, but with authenticity; don't ever lose your true colors. Get to know your audience; know their background; know what makes them tick. Does your client come from a certain industry or background? Colleagues from various departments often have varying outlooks on organizational needs and importance. Adjust your style accordingly. A casual chat will differ from a formal boardroom presentation. If something's not working, be ready to

adjust, but again, stay true to yourself. Authenticity and adaptability can coexist. You don't have to choose one or the other.
3. **Avoiding difficult conversations.** Nobody likes tough conversations, but ducking them only makes them worse. Develop skills in handling conflict and giving constructive feedback.
4. **Failing to manage stress.** Letting stress get the better of us on a regular basis is a surefire way to damage executive presence. Find ways to manage stress and keep your work-life balance in check.

How to Stand Out

Finally, here are some tips for standing out in a professional environment.

1. **Be well prepared for meetings and presentations.** As a matter of fact, be the most prepared person in the room.
2. **Speak up** with insights that add value and contribute meaningful conversation, but don't be a know-it-all.
3. **Take initiative** on projects and challenges.
4. **Be a problem solver**, not a problem pointer outer.
5. **Build and maintain strong relationships** in every part of your organization. You never know where your next opportunity might come from.
6. **Consistently deliver high-quality work.**

>>><<<

Be the most prepared person in the room.

>>><<<

Growth and Self-Investment

Developing executive presence is kind of a journey. Executive presence isn't just something that you achieve and then forget about. It doesn't happen overnight. It's about consistently applying these strategies and learning from your experiences. It also requires continual growth, self-investment, and nurturing. It's like growing a plant: you've got to keep the water flowing.

Why bother? Continual self-improvement keeps your skills and knowledge up-to-date. You want to stay sharp. The business world isn't standing still, and neither should you. Moreover, self-improvement—which people sometimes call lifelong learning—demonstrates your commitment to personal and professional growth. It shows everyone that you're serious. It helps you roll with the punches and remain adaptable to ever-changing business environments and landscapes. And it certainly makes you more credible and influential—and who doesn't want that?

Strategies for Continual Development

What are some strategies for continual learning and development?

1. **Seek feedback regularly.** Don't be shy about asking for feedback. Although it can be scary, it is gold. Ask your colleagues, your boss, or a mentor. Asking people to give you feedback communicates that you value their opinion and trust their advice. Hence it helps to build your authority, credibility, likeability—and your executive presence.

2. **Attend workshops and seminars.** With today's virtual environment, you can attend webinars. You can attend full six-hour courses or multiday courses virtually. You don't even have to leave your office or your house. That being said, you can also go out and find live, in-person classes that may enable you to focus better.
3. **Take in knowledge.** Read, read, and then read some more. Stay on top of what's happening in your industry. Read books about communication strategies and leadership. Soak it all in. Stay abreast of the latest thinking in leadership, especially in your industry.
4. **Practice public speaking.** Many people feel apprehensive about this suggestion. But look for chances to present at meetings or conferences. It's like a workout for your communication muscles. You may not like it at first, and it may even burn a little, but it's good for you in the long run.
5. **Engage in self-reflection.** Don't forget to look inward. Take time regularly to reflect on your strengths and weaknesses. Identify the work that you need to do, and then do it. It will serve you well in terms of gravitas, communication, and even appearance.

Goal Setting

If you want to make real progress, you have to get specific. Identify specific aspects of your executive presence that you want to improve. Pick out the exact areas that need some work, and be honest with yourself.

We've already covered SWOT analysis in chapter 2. As you'll remember, SWOT stands for *strengths, weaknesses, opportunities*, and *threats*. SWOT yourself. Identify your strengths, identify your weaknesses, and identify opportunities that you can take to deal with them. Be honest about possible threats to seizing those opportunities.

If you SWOT yourself and you do it the right way—honestly—it's going to sting a little, and that's OK. It should, because only when you are honest with yourself can you set smart goals that will assist you professionally, personally, and even in regard to your organization.

In dealing with goals, we've already come across the acronym SMART. Goals must be *specific, measurable, achievable, relevant*, and *time-bound*. (In some versions, like the one we discussed earlier, the A stands for *agreed upon*.) Don't be vague; be detailed. SMART goals: be *specific* about the goal. Identify how you're going to *measure* success. Make sure the goal is *achievable* and relevant to the situation. And put a *timer* on it.

How will I measure success? Often by using key performance indicators (KPIs). That is a good way to set a goal, measure it, and meet it. Create your action plan and have concrete steps. Know what has to happen for you to achieve these goals and get ready to make those steps work for you. Regularly review and adjust your goals as the need arises: goal setting is not a "set it and forget it activity." Review your goals regularly and adjust them.

Self-Investment

Invest in yourself. That means allocating time and resources for your professional development and growth. This requires carving time out of your schedule. It might mean saying no to some things—involving time, money, or other investments—in order to say yes to your growth. It could be time, it could be money, it could be a lot of different things.

Again, balance is important, but don't use balance as an excuse to forgo the investment you make in yourself. Consider working with a coach or a mentor. Sometimes an outside perspective can work wonders.

Be brave enough to step outside of your comfort zone, because that's where the magic will happen. That's where you're going to see the most growth, learning, and forward motion in your personal and professional life. Recognize also that self-investment is an ongoing process: it's a marathon, not a sprint.

The Case of Kara

As we close this chapter, let's look at the case study of a woman named Kara. She wanted to develop a strong executive presence, but she had some obstacles to overcome. She began her career as a software engineer at a midsize tech company. While technically proficient, she initially struggled to make her voice heard in meetings, and she often felt overlooked for high-profile projects. Recognizing the need to develop her executive presence, Kara embarked on a journey of self-improvement.

First, she addressed her communication skills. Kara joined Toastmasters—an organization designed to help people improve their communication skills—to enhance her public speaking abilities. She practiced articulating her ideas clearly and concisely, in both meetings and presentations. Next, she worked on her body language. She hired a coach to improve her nonverbal communication, focusing on maintaining eye contact, using confident gestures, and adopting a strong posture. In the area of strategic thinking, Kara sought opportunities to contribute companywide to a variety of different initiatives. This demonstrated her ability to think beyond her immediate role. Kara put away any thought of, "That's not my department; that's not my job." She embraced multifunctional teams and cross-functional initiatives. Additionally, she networked. She built relationships across departments and hierarchies, establishing herself as a connector within the organization. She became someone that everyone knew, and for good, positive reasons.

Kara also invested in her image, purchasing a polished, professional wardrobe that aligned with her company's culture while reflecting her personal style. Finally, in the area of emotional intelligence, she developed her ability to read room dynamics, and she adapted her communication style to different audiences as the need arose.

Kara did all of these things, not overnight, but over the course of two years. Her efforts paid off. She was selected to lead a critical project, which showcased her technical skills and her leadership abilities. Senior executives began to seek her input on strategic decisions. She was invited to represent the company at industry conferences. Finally, she received a promotion to senior engineer and was put on a fast track for a management role.

Kara's story illustrates how, with dedication and with the right strategies, anyone can cultivate a strong executive presence and stand out in their professional environment.

Key Points in This Chapter

In this chapter, we've explored a number of aspects of developing executive presence. We began by talking about the foundational aspects: the three pillars of executive presence. Then we moved on to mastering communication and influence. We talked about the importance of professional image and networking, not only within your organization, but in your industry. We talked about pitfalls to avoid and the dos and don'ts of cultivating success. Finally, we looked at continual growth and the importance of self-investment.

FIVE

Optimal Communication Styles

This chapter will address optimal communication styles. It will discuss the principal styles: passive, aggressive, and assertive and show why the last is by far the most preferable. It will discuss the four Rs of assertiveness as well as the ABCs of rational thinking and removing obstacles to communication. It will discuss barriers in self-concept and methods for eliminating them. The chapter will focus on active listening as a way of improving communication. Some assertiveness scripts will also be presented as a way of enhancing effective communication. The different forms of communication—verbal, email, or in writing—and their best uses will be covered, as will the crucial role of nonverbal communication.

Basic Styles

Managers generally fall into one of three groups: *aggressive* communicators, *passive* communicators, or *assertive* communicators. Those that are too aggressive may succeed in completing short-term goals, but often struggle to maintain positive relationships with their employees over time. Managers that are too passive have no problem in building relationships but find it challenging to motivate others and solve problems in order to move the team forward.

Each of us is naturally born to be either more passive or more aggressive. Furthermore, depending on whom you're communicating with, you can be more of a passive communicator (as with your boss) or more of an aggressive communicator or an assertive communicator.

It is your goal to use assertive communication more and more over time; and as you practice, this does happen.

> **It is your goal to use assertive communication.**

To help you discover the style that comes most naturally to you, let's run through each style. As you read the description of each one, take special note of situations where you might have acted more aggressively or passively. Certain occasions will trigger you to use a more assertive style; others will trigger you to be more aggressive or passive. At this point, we want to focus on times when you become more aggressive or passive.

Let's start with the passive communicator. Passive communicators want to be liked. They typically think of themselves as likable or friendly. They are not comfortable with conflict, so they avoid it when possible; they will often silence their own thoughts or feelings just to avoid conflict. This person doesn't like to rock the boat or is afraid that people will be upset with them. As speakers, they tend not to be respectful of their own words and often they feel they're getting walked on by other people. The passive communicator might have thoughts such as, "I won't offer my opinion," "I want my employees to like me," or "It's not my place to speak up." They may think that nice people don't disagree.

There's nothing wrong with being a nice, friendly person.

There are some occasions when these qualities should take precedence. But this type of communicator suffers from a number of disadvantages. They can find themselves acting like a yes person to upper management. Yet they are often seen by upper management as ineffective leaders, because this communication style often doesn't get things done in a timely manner: they're always waiting to see what others want to do before deciding what to do themselves. Passive managers create possibilities for miscommunication because they often fail to set clear expectations. In addition, there's no skill development here, because these managers tend not to give constructive criticism, and subordinates don't know what to improve upon.

Of course, no manager is 100 percent passive. Consider: in the last thirty days, under what circumstances did you behave more passively? Take a moment and jot them down.

Next, let's look at the aggressive communicator. Characteristic behaviors of this type include whining, intimidating, and overpowering just to get their way. As speakers, they do not respect the listeners' needs.

Often and unfortunately, these communicators get their way by belittling, degrading, or humiliating others. As you can probably imagine, this type of behavior can accomplish their goals. However, these goals ultimately reflect only that person's perception. There's no input on what, how, or when these goals might be achieved by those they are communicating with. This style can also trigger retaliation in the form of passive-aggressive behavior, such as agreeing to the goal but not working to achieve it, say by missing deadlines or failing to deliver information as agreed. The aggressive manager gets people to say yes but frequently cannot make them perform.

> The aggressive manager gets people to say yes but frequently cannot make them perform.

Often a nonaggressive manager can turn aggressive when they're stressed, deadlines get closer, or upper management is pressing them. Keep this in mind as you look for times when you are more likely to communicate in an aggressive manner.

The manager with an aggressive style demotivates the team both as individuals and as a group, resulting in lower productivity and lower-quality output. The aggressive manager may be respected by upper management, but that is quickly lost when the team begins to complain about the manager and the department has a high turnover rate.

Again, no manager is 100 percent aggressive, so consider the circumstances in the last thirty days under which you behaved more aggressively. Take a moment, and jot those down.

> **Assertive communication is the ability to honestly express your feelings, opinions, and attitudes in a way that respects the rights of yourself and others.**

Ideally, as a manager, you want to communicate in a way that respects the needs of both the communicator and the listeners. This is assertive communication: the ability to honestly express your feelings, opinions, and attitudes in a way that respects the rights of yourself and others. When you use assertive communication, you show a higher level of confidence. The listener feels heard and respected. As a result, they're more apt to admit mistakes, change their mind, and more openly accept criticism. This allows a manager to move a person forward, advance a team, and build a successful organization.

Assertive managers recognize that their own opinions have value, and they express those opinions in a clear and respectful way. They also know how to punch the right buttons and motivate without being too pushy and overbearing and without begging or pleading. This balanced management style generates the most out of employees and helps everyone get the job done right every time.

Managers can confuse assertive with passive and aggressive styles. To illustrate the difference, let's look at a few comparisons, starting with beliefs. Passive communicators put their needs below those of others, resulting in lower self-esteem and self-respect and a belief that "I'm not OK." They

> **Management Styles and Beliefs**
> 1. Passive: "I'm not OK": lose-win
> 2. Aggressive: "You're not OK": win-lose
> 3. Assertive: "You're OK and I'm OK": win-win

may feel they're not good enough without knowing why. In fact, there's nothing to validate this belief.

The more aggressive communicator clearly places their needs above those of others, diminishing their self-esteem, disrespecting them, and giving them the feeling they're not OK. Often aggressive communicators are not even aware they're doing this.

Assertive communicators have high self-esteem and confidence; they don't have to diminish others' self-esteem to boost their own. They're balanced people, behaving in a manner that respects themselves as well as those they work with. They treat others as equals and communicate that "I'm OK and you're OK."

Another way to clearly see the difference in communication is through how these different types handle their emotions. Passive managers often refrain from sharing their feelings and hold it all in. Over time they build up frustration, and they've been known to suddenly explode over the smallest things, leaving people wondering what happened.

The aggressive communicator, on the other hand, lets it all hang out and often quickly expresses their negative feelings with no filters. You quickly know when they're not happy. As a result, employees are often reluctant to approach them for fear of their reactions.

Assertive communicators use filters in expressing their feelings. For many, this is not easy. Neither the passive nor the aggressive person has this trait naturally, so it has to be learned. This takes practice and time, and it starts with acknowledging that something must be said and crafting a tactful way to say it.

Often assertive communicators turn into aggressive or passive communicators when they're squeezed or put into a stressful situation. To further clarify, let's look at how each communicator behaves in a tough situation.

Let's start with a scenario. You're the boss and you're responsible for turning a report in to upper management. Your employee was supposed to produce the report for you, and he is turning in the report late. Your manager has asked you about it. If you are a passive or aggressive communicator, you are more likely to resort to blaming. The passive communicator will do it through a subtle statement like, "Oh, John didn't get the report to me on time," where the aggressive communicator might be direct and straight to the point, saying, "It's John's fault: he got the report to me late." Although John might have gotten the report in, the assertive communicator would say, "I'm still working on the report and will have it done by Friday." They take personal responsibility. Probably this manager would have approached John the day before the report was due and ask for an update. If the delay was going to affect the deliverable, they would have communicated with their own manager. There would be no need for blame, because everything was communicated.

In the end, the passive communicator settles for a lose-win situation, whereby they sacrifice to let the other person win. The aggressive communicator positions for a win-lose situation to make sure their needs are taken care of. An assertive communicator seeks a win-win, so there is a balance and open communication.

Assertive managers have less conflict, because they present ideas in a clear, effective way, using tact and professionalism. They are able to diffuse volatile situations faster, while motivating others and maintaining positive relationships with their team.

The Four Rs of Assertiveness

Assertive managers have their foundation in their beliefs rather than merely using the words and actions of assertive communicators. If your spoken words are mechanical or insincere, they're worthless. When you have founded your development on solid beliefs, your communication is no longer a choice that can be challenged by emotions on a day-to-day basis.

The most effective managers employ the principles of assertive management. This belief system is epitomized in the four Rs of assertion.

The first R is *respect* for yourself. Respect is the basis of all relationships. If you have low self-respect or self-esteem, it's very difficult for you to respect others and it's equally unlikely that others will respect you. Others will treat you as they see you treating yourself. Children get their self-esteem from external sources, usually parents, teachers, or relatives. When a child does something right, he or she is rewarded with praise and develops a sense of self-worth or self-esteem.

> **The Four Rs of Assertiveness**
> 1. Respect
> 2. Rights
> 3. Responsibility
> 4. Rational thinking

By the time we're adults, our self-esteem comes from internal sources. It's not an event in and of itself that affects our self-esteem, but our intrinsic reaction to the event. For example, it isn't getting laid off as such that affects our self-esteem: it's our internal reaction to getting laid off. We might think, "I must not be good enough to be kept around. They were probably looking for a way to get rid of me anyway."

Unfortunately, what you think of yourself affects what other people think of you. If you don't think you're good enough to be retained as an employee, how are you going to get a new job?

People with low self-respect and low self-esteem have unrealistic expectations of themselves. Many believe they must be perfect; when they are not, they think they will never measure up, and that's why they aren't as good as others. But nobody's perfect. A perfect person has never existed.

In order to replace perfectionistic thinking, set realistic expectations. It is OK *not* to be perfect. Find out what is acceptable, and aim for that. Instead of using your standards, use the standards of those you are working for. Let them tell you what is good enough. If you make a mistake, it's OK; correct the mistake, learn from it, and learn how you can be better. There's no need to beat yourself up. Others will forgive your mistake and give you another chance. You need to forgive yourself and give yourself another chance as well.

In the self-improvement classic *The Four Agreements* by Don Miguel Ruiz, the fourth agreement is to always do your best. Your best is going to change from moment to moment. It will be different when you're healthy from when you're sick. Simply do your best under any circumstances, and you will avoid self-judgment, self-blame, and regret.

◇◇

Always do your best.

◇◇

This also brings us to "better than" thinking: the notion that one person is better than another. If someone had a $20 bill and could give it to you, would you want it? Does it have value? Certainly. What if this person crumpled up that $20 bill? Does it still have value? Of course. If the person dropped it on the floor and stepped on it, would you still want it? Yes, because it still has value.

The same is true for us as humans. Even if we have been disregarded, shuffled around, and treated unfairly, we still have an innate value, just as that $20 bill is worth $20 regardless of its condition. Every human being has value regardless of their circumstances. No one person is innately better than another. No $20 bill is better than any other $20 bill. We are all equally valuable: different but valuable.

An aggressive person will find reasons why *you* are not as good, and a passive person will find reasons why *they* are not as good. But as Eleanor Roosevelt said, no one can make you feel inferior without your consent. Ultimately, you are in control of how you feel and how others treat you.

The second R in the four Rs of assertion is the *rights* of yourself and others. When you elevate your own self-respect, you begin to respect your own rights and those of others. Many times self-development and assertiveness are hindered by thinking that others' rights come before one's own. As children, we are taught to let other kids play with our toys, share our candy, and let guests have first dibs on everything. This mindset of putting others' needs first tends to stick with us as we grow up. It hurts our self-esteem and self-respect when applied in work life.

The third R in the four Rs of assertion is *responsibility* for self and others. Rights and responsibility go hand in hand. How do we balance exercising our rights with our responsibilities to others? Assertiveness becomes aggression when it is used without concern or responsibility towards others, their situations, or their feelings. As a manager, you are responsible to employees by being clear about expectations and consequences, but you are not responsible for the choices the employees make afterwards. You are assertive when your responsibility to yourself is balanced with your responsibility to others. The key term here is *to* others, not *for* others.

To better understand the separation of rights and responsibilities, let's take an example. You have the right to go ahead with your own job in your own way, once the objectives and restraints have been clarified. This is your right. With that comes a responsibility for staying within the limits established. You have a right, but it is accompanied by a responsibility.

The fourth and final R in the four Rs of assertion is *rational thinking*. It will shed light on how irrational beliefs can lead to negative consequences and how refocusing based on rational thought can contribute to positive outcomes.

As we've already seen, it's not a given event itself that hurts us, but our response to it. Many behavioral psychologists use a method called the *ABCs of rational thinking* as a way to analyze events that took place, our reaction to those events, and the consequences of our reactions.

Let's say that rational thinking is logical thinking and irrational thinking is not based on logical reason or includes significant assumptions that make the thinking illogical. For example, if someone disagrees with you, it would be rational to think they do not believe the same thing you believe; it would be irrational to think it is a personal attack on you.

Let's break this down. *A* refers to the *activating event*. What happened? What started things off? What would a camera have seen? *B* refers to your *beliefs* about the activating event. What did you tell yourself about the event after it happened? What are your feelings or reactions to what happened? *C* refers to *consequences*. How did you react to your perception of the event? What behaviors did you display?

The ABCs of Rational Thinking

A. Activating event
B. Beliefs resulting from event
C. Consequence

Let's look at these ABCs in action. Meet Robert. He's a young man who tends to doubt himself. One day on a lunch break, Robert passes a coworker in the hallway. He smiles at the coworker and says hello, but the coworker does not return his greeting.

Let's analyze this situation using the ABC format. Let's look at first A, the activating event. What started things off? The coworker passed Robert in the hallway without acknowledging him. That's the event. A camera would have seen that.

B is our belief about the activating event. In this case, Robert might have had the following thoughts: "He's ignoring me. He doesn't like me. I could end up without friends forever, and that would be terrible. To be happy and feel worthwhile, I need people to like me. Nobody wants to be my friend, so I must be a worthless person."

C has to do with the consequences: because of Robert's irrational feelings about the event, he feels worthless and depressed. As a result, his behavior changes. He starts to avoid people.

Someone with high self-confidence uses more rational thinking in relation to the same event. Let's take a look at how that would play out. Thomas has higher self-esteem and sees his own reactions and thought processes. Again, A, the activating event, is a coworker passing him in the hall without responding when Thomas said hello.

Thomas thinks this way: "He didn't ignore me deliberately. He must not have heard me. He might have had something on his mind." Thomas does not take being ignored as a personal attack: the other person must have had something on their mind, so Thomas doesn't change his behavior. He realizes, "This isn't about me."

These examples show how two different ways of reacting to the same event can lead to different consequences and different sets of behavior. Irrational consequences are counterproductive, while those based in rational thought lead to enhanced relationships and higher productivity.

Think rationally. Not everyone reacts the same way to the same events. If an event causes an irrational reaction, stop and analyze the consequences and beliefs behind them. Once you shed rational light on an irrational response, you can move forward productively rather than letting the emotion wreak havoc. Show respect for others and take responsibility for yourself.

Removing Barriers to Communication

Communicating assertively can help you become a better leader. However, mastering this type of communication takes not only practice but knowledge about the obstacles that stand in your way, why those obstacles are there, and how to break through them.

Numerous real and perceived barriers can distort a message, whether you're the listener or the speaker. The first barrier is your perception or interpretation of what is being said. Each of us has layers of experience, education, culture, religion, age, and other factors through which we filter information. No two people ever hear the same message the same way. Have you ever sat in a meeting where someone sitting next to you had a completely different perception of what

> **Three Barriers in Self-Concept**
> 1. "If I assert myself, others will be angry or upset with me."
> 2. "If my assertive communication hurts others, I'm responsible for their feelings."
> 3. "I must avoid making mistakes or asking questions that might make me look ignorant."

happened during this meeting? Maybe they were frustrated or shocked by the outcome, while your response was that it was no big deal.

Much of how we hear things and how we think people will react has to do with our own self-perception and personal needs. We perceive things in a way that meets our needs at that moment. In the example of the meeting, the person who was frustrated by the outcome was probably more personally affected by it than the person who was not. The outcome might mean extra work for the first person and the same or less work for the other person, or maybe the latter had already heard about it, while it was news to the first.

Frequently what blocks us from communicating assertively is our own self-concept. *Self-concept* refers to characteristics and attributes we believe that we have. In other words, our own theory about ourselves can create barriers to becoming more assertive. Certain insecurities may skew our self-perception.

There are many barriers based on our self-concept that prevent us from communicating assertively. Let's look at the three most significant ones.

1. The belief that "if I assert myself, others will be angry or upset with me." The truth is, it is part of your job as the leader to make decisions. Your employees and colleagues expect and need you to do so. Because people have different perspectives, not everyone will respond to your decisions in the same way. However, if you assert yourself appropriately, communicating clearly and with respect for your own position as well as for those around you, you should not feel responsible for other people's reactions. More often than not, if you consistently communicate with your team and colleagues in an assertive manner, you'll gain a level of respect that will lead to consistent and committed cooperation. It is less important that they wholeheartedly agree with your decision than that they respect you enough to honor your decision.

    Let's look at an example. Jim, one of your employees, has interrupted you four times this morning for something that is not urgent. By the fifth time, you've had it. You want to say to Jim, "You've been interrupting me all day. Can't you see I'm busy? If you interrupt me one more time, I'm going to scream." You're beyond frustrated, but you're afraid that if you say something wrong, you're going to upset Jim.

    How do you handle this situation? As an assertive communicator, you might calmly say, "Jim, before you ask your question, I'm in the middle of finishing something important. I'm running short on time. If it's something that can wait until tomorrow, I'd greatly appreciate it, but if it's urgent, let's go ahead and talk about it right now."

This scenario is respectful of both parties involved. You state the reality of the situation, identify your needs, and ask for those needs to be respected. At the same time, you're respectful of Jim's needs, letting him know that if it really must be done right now, you'll take a minute for him.

2. "If my assertive communication hurts others, I'm responsible for their feelings." The truth is, most people are going to appreciate your clear communication and your empathy. If you are truly communicating in an assertive manner, you should not take on the burden of responsibility for the way others feel or react. In the example of Jim, you can't let your worry about his feelings stop you from getting your work done. By interrupting, Jim is not communicating assertively: he's not respecting your needs. Part of being an assertive manager is to set the expectation that those you work with will also communicate assertively. Once you've been clear with Jim regarding what you need and helped him understand that you do want to hear what he has to say, it's out of your hands. How Jim reacts is Jim's responsibility.

3. "At all costs, I must avoid making mistakes or asking questions that might make me look ignorant or make it seem as if I don't know what I'm doing." The truth is, if you lack information, it is better to admit it and get the information so you can make informed decisions. If you've made a mistake, it's better to admit it and figure out how to fix it than to blame somebody else or let it snowball into a nightmare. Everybody has questions, and everybody makes mistakes. Your employees and peers will respect you more if you can show your human side.

When you allow yourself to be human and make mistakes, you also give your team permission not to have to be perfect and open the door for them to ask questions. The standard you set for yourself becomes the standard you set for others.

Improving Self-Concept

Many of these self-concepts can be improved by developing positive self-respect. Once you accept that you are a vulnerable person who is not perfect, you can take specific steps to increase your self-esteem and self-respect on a daily basis.

Start by focusing on your strengths. Since no one is great at everything, the best way to build your self-esteem is to establish what you are great at and focus on that. You may conclude that you're really good at strategy but not as good at minute details. As a big-picture thinker, you might feel bad about yourself if you were to focus on minutiae. Instead, to increase your self-esteem, you want to focus on what you are good at and delegate the tasks that you're not good at to other people. The old adage of working on the weakness has proven to be ineffective. You can work forever on getting better with minutiae, but you may never get better than a 5 on a scale of 1 to 10, whereas if you focus on strategy, you can go from an 8 to a 10 and really excel.

Sometimes you have to get creative on how to make a weakness irrelevant. Albert Einstein knew he was challenged in terms of fashion, so he found outfits that looked good, bought multiples of them, and wore the same type of outfit every day.

Now you might have a little voice in your head saying, "But you *should* have . . ." *Should* is a value judgment: "You *should* do this. You *shouldn't* do that." It lowers your self-esteem and self-respect. Instead, substitute the word *could* for *should* and emphasize it as a choice: "I could do that," not "I should," and follow that statement with "I will" or "I won't." This puts you in charge of your life and enables you to act by choice rather than reacting helplessly to the actions of those around you. This in turn leads to greater self-confidence, self-esteem, and reduced stress and anxiety.

The use of should lowers your self-esteem.

The little voice that tries to sabotage you—the one that tries to *should* on you—needs to be reprogrammed. It sometimes says things that are not empowering and need to be altered. It is the voice of thoughts that have been repeated over and over again. When you hear that little voice say something, evaluate it and ask yourself, "Is that true, or is that the voice of someone else who really didn't know me?" For example, one woman had a father that used to say, "You'll never grow up to be anything." That is what her voice said. She'd make a mistake, and it'd say, "See? You'll never grow up to be anything." She would go for promotions, and that voice would keep her even from submitting the application. She learned to reprogram it to say, "I can do anything I want." Later she became vice president of the company.

To reprogram that voice, start by recognizing it. When it speaks, say, "Stop," and say the statement you want it to learn. You might say, "Stop. I can do anything I want," and over time, that voice will change. This takes time and effort, but the results are amazing.

The words and phrases used by your little voice have been accumulated over time. If you were raised in a less than positive environment, your voice probably has several messages that need to be replaced. The best way to replace them all is to engage in self-development learning. This can take the form of a book or listening to audios. Many find that when they exercise, listening to a development audio helps them achieve both better physical health and better mental health. Exercising is also a great way to improve your self-esteem, since it promotes weight loss and better muscle tone. Exercise releases endorphins: internally produced chemicals that have a positive impact on your mind and body and help you feel much better about yourself.

Other Barriers to Communication

Other barriers to communication include lack of planning, different reality perspectives, using assumptions, and poor word choice. Many of these can be corrected with two techniques.

The first is listening. It is one of the skills that often requires the most practice, but it is arguably the most important managerial skill to have. Many of us operate in a fast-moving environment, and our lives and jobs force us to multitask. In order to listen appropriately, you must show the other person that you care about what they have to say and are doing your best to understand their message, You must drop what you're doing, stop, and give that person your full attention.

While most of us can hear, few of us can effectively listen. There's a big difference: hearing is merely receiving sound, whereas listening is proactive and requires considerable effort. To listen effectively in person, you must physically turn yourself towards the speaker and make eye contact to show that you are ready to receive the message. If you are on the phone, this readiness is indicated by verbal clues like "Yeah" or "Uh-huh." Most of us indicate our readiness to listen by nodding our heads even when we are on the phone and the other person can't see us. We also often use verbal clues to let the speaker know we understand and that we want them to continue.

Nevertheless, overuse of nodding and vocal cues can come across as insecure, almost as hurry-up body language, making the speaker think you're not listening to them; as a result, they will rush to deliver the message before you give up on them. Pay close attention to your nonverbal language and your listening.

You should listen for feelings as well as facts. Use your eyes, your intuition, and your ears to obtain the entire message. Someone's words can be betrayed by their actions. Listen for the main idea, disregarding sidetracks. Some people take sidetracks as part of their everyday conversation. Others take sidetracks when they're emotionally charged. Ignore sidetracks and focus on the main point they're trying to make. Listen without interrupting. Especially when we're in a hurry, we tend to jump in and finish other people's thoughts, thinking we know what they're trying to say. We're often wrong, which creates a common miscommunication barrier. Not only is this disrespectful of the other person, it wastes time. The speaker often has to backtrack, regroup, and try again. Save time by listening well and actively in the first place.

Listen for feelings as well as facts.

The second technique for overcoming communication barriers is to prepare feedback and paraphrase after the speaker is done—but never prepare your feedback while the speaker is speaking. It takes your attention away from their message and will most likely make you miss some important aspect of it. Focus and refocus your attention on the speaker until they are finished. When they are, reflect back what you have heard in terms of feeling and content. You might say something like, "It sounds like you're a little frustrated in this situation. What I hear you saying is, your coworkers are not providing you with the information you need in a timely manner. Is that correct?" This type of feedback not only clarifies the message but also acknowledges the speaker's feelings and allows you to respond appropriately the first time. This technique allows the speaker to confirm your interpretation, reducing barriers to communication and increasing cooperation.

Assertiveness Scripts

Becoming more assertive is going to take some conscious effort, and having a model to follow makes this transition a little easier. So let's look at the three components of assertiveness. This model can be used in endless situations and especially those where heightened emotions are involved.

> **Three Components of Assertiveness**
> 1. Acknowledge the other person.
> 2. State the problem.
> 3. Request what you want or invite feedback.

The first step is to validate or acknowledge the other person, then to make a statement of the problem; and lastly, to make a request or invite feedback.

Let's break this down even further. In the validation step, you're saying something that acknowledges the other person's feeling but does not buy into their emotion. You are empathizing but not sympathizing.

Empathizing is like being on the shore and encouraging the other person to row to the shore; sympathizing is hopping in the boat with them. Empathy shows the other person that you're not trying to pick a fight but that you have heard what they are saying.

To avoid getting emotionally involved with another's feelings, use statements like, "What I hear you saying is . . ." or "What I see happening is . . ." These introductory statements allow you to make an observation rather than an accusation. One example of validation might be, "I know that you get nervous when a big report is due to upper management." This is phrased as an "I" statement. An "I" statement focuses on the problem, not on accusing or blaming. "I" statements help prevent the use of absolutes and exaggerations and of questions other than for the purpose of retrieving specific information. You can start "I" statements with, "I feel"; "I know"; "I need."

The next step is to state the problem: describe your difficulty or dissatisfaction with the situation and why it needs to change. An example is, " I saw several spelling mistakes and errors in the report that was just turned in." Again, remember these are "I" statements.

The last step is to request what you want. The core request needs to be specific. What changes do you want them to make? For example, "From now on, before turning in a big report, I'd like to proofread it so we catch the errors before upper management sees them."

Another option in this step is to ask for feedback. This is helpful when you've identified a specific behavior and you're asking the employee to make a specific change. When you ask the employee to suggest a solution, they're much more likely to implement it than when you tell them what to do. An example: "What can you do to arrive on time from now on?"

Note that this is the employee's problem, not yours, and the employee is solely responsible for resolving their issues about arriving on time. Assertive communicators do not take ownership of another person's problems. They may offer suggestions, but only when asked. This keeps the conversation open, mutual, and respectful.

Another variation of this script is, "I feel ___ when you ___." This allows a speaker to communicate their feelings in a constructive manner that is not accusing or blaming. Take the example of an employee who interrupts the manager during an important meeting with upper management. An assertive conversation after the meeting might start with, "Joe, I felt disrespected when you corrected me in front of my superiors. I recognize I might be making an error, but I would prefer if you would hold your comments until afterwards and tell me in a private meeting." This script provides the words to express your emotions in an assertive manner, so that you're neither walking on the other person nor letting them walk on yours.

Scenarios

Let's apply these scripts to a few scenarios.

First is a situation where your star employee, Michael, has been working very hard and requests Friday off, but it will cause great inconvenience for the rest of the team. How can you address this in an assertive manner? You can try this: "Michael, I understand you want Friday off. Unfortunately, this will put the team behind on the project. Could you take a day after the deadline or perhaps work overtime to help us stay on schedule?" By addressing the request in this manner, you respect it, but you also respect the inconvenience that it will cause the team and ask for a solution.

Next scenario: You have an employee, Abby, who is late for the third time this week. What can you say to address this in an assertive manner? One option: "Abby, I see that you have arrived after 8:30 three times this week. I expect you to be on time." If you've addressed this problem before and it's still happening, you might need to ask Abby to provide you with a solution for resolving this challenge. It might sound something like this: "Abby, this is the third time this week you've punched in after 8:30. It is important that you be on time. What can you change to make sure you arrive and punch in before 8:30?" This way, you're asking the employee to provide a solution, so they're much more likely to implement it.

It's also important to monitor your words. Some words push hidden buttons and cause resistance. These words include *can't*, *need*, *have*, and *should*. Psychologically, when we hear them, we start to build a wall of resistance. When someone says, "You *have to* . . ." part of you wants to rebel and say, "I don't *have to* do anything." By replacing these words with other, less charged words, your message will be easier on the listener's ear and reduce resistance. Replace *can't* with *won't*, *have to* with *choose to*, *need* with *want*. As already suggested, instead of *should*, use *could*.

Being assertive is more than words and scripts. You also want to put yourself in complete control of a situation by getting to the facts and having the details at hand, rather than having to wing it with half of the story. Our behavior can turn aggressive when we try to compensate for our lack of knowledge. Our emotions tempt us to make quick decisions based on superficial information, which may not reflect the true nature of the problem.

Take for example, a manager who assumes that the poor appearance of a store is due to an employee's lack of effort. The manager fails to consider that several store employees have been terminated because of financial situations, while the store's workload has remained the same. Without all the information, it's easy to jump to conclusions that turns mole-hills into mountains. Gather and confirm information before making decisions. The assertive manager asks enough questions to understand the situation before trying to solve the problem.

Next is anticipating the other person's behavior: when you do so, you can begin to prepare your response, which allows even the most reactive person to stay in control in difficult situations.

Focus on problems, not personalities. As managers, we may have team members whose style rubs us the wrong way. When you are providing constructive criticism, focusing on the problem rather than the person will greatly reduce resistance. This is much easier said than done. It is easier to say, "Stop being so social and get to work," but this is focusing on personality. It is better to focus on the problem: the fact that the individual is not getting their work done.

Focus on problems, not personalities.

Whenever dealing with any issue that might have emotional content, the twenty-four-hour rule should be in effect. Don't send any email message, letter, memo, or report to others that you haven't had at least a day to reflect upon to make sure its content communicates the facts and tone you desire.

Employees do not take jobs with the expectation that they will be overlooked, ignored, or insignificant. Employees want to be liked and respected by their peers and proud of their employer. Management's challenge is to maintain and develop employees' enthusiasm and commitment even during times of stress.

As we've seen, mistakes are part of the growth process, and falling short and correcting course are regular occurrences in business and life. If you know the person is likely to become aggressive, practice your response, which prepares you for the conversation that you're going to have. The benefit is that you're not under pressure and can rehearse the response.

Communicating Boundaries and Expectations

In order to empower employees to achieve and accomplish at the highest level, you as the manager must clearly set and communicate boundaries and expectations and hold everyone accountable to them. Managers who fail to clearly define and consistently enforce boundaries are in trouble with their employees. They are not mind readers, and if you have not communicated your expectations, it is your fault as manager.

It is easy to think that it's enough to send an email or a memo stating your expectations, but when communication is directed towards everyone, it's really directed towards no one. The lack of specificity enables each recipient to avoid taking personal responsibility. Each may feel that they have met the expectations. As a consequence, these communications fail to get the desired result and can aggravate an already touchy work environment. Group communications are perfect for providing general information, education, and praise, but they should not be used for individual direction or criticism.

What should you do to establish clear expectations? Meet with employees face to face. The meaning and intent of written words without the context of a physical presence are often misunderstood and can lead to confusion and conflict. There is no substitute for looking someone in the eye and seeing their reaction in order to clarify content and assure comprehension and agreement. Some managers hide behind memos and notes, but successful leaders seek personal commitment and build bridges of trust, mutual respect, and shared experience.

Also make sure that you're communicating clearly. Assign tasks directly. People work best when they know what's expected of them. Assertive managers identify goals and measure them in simple, understandable terms. Assign responsibility unequivocally, and confirm that the information is understood. Assertive managers follow up and give corrective input to ensure that everyone is on the same page and is working towards the same objectives.

Next, you need to hold employees accountable to the expectations. This sounds easy until you try it; then suddenly you find that there are more exceptions than you can imagine. These are not easy decisions, but consistency will empower your employees to respect you and will establish standards in your organization.

>>
Choose your battles carefully.
>>

Finally, choose your battles carefully. An effective manager knows it's better to lose the battle and win the war. Choosing not to fight a battle you know you can't win is a sign of wisdom and not weakness.

Effective Communication Skills

Assertiveness does not just happen and can be completely ineffective without the skills required for effective communication. Skill areas include being results-oriented as well as a correct use of statements, voice, and body language.

All communications have results, but was the result the one you desired? Business relationships, especially those between superior and subordinates, can get rocky if the manager does not have a clear vision of the outcome they desire from the communication; this is when a normally assertive manager can turn aggressive or passive. To remain assertive, decide before you have the conversation: what results do you want to achieve? Too often, inexperienced managers will provide criticism to an employee while forgetting to ask them for specific behavioral changes. Without asking for a specific change, the chances of getting a change are greatly reduced.

When asking for a change, a common mistake is to use questions instead of statements. A question is assertive if you require information or when you want to make a request.

However, too often we ask a question when we should be making a statement: for example, asking an employee is, "Why do you always arrive late?" This question, stated in a *you* format, is accusatory and blaming. Do you really want to know why they're always late, or do you just want them to arrive on time? Instead of asking the question, make a statement: "I expect you to be on time." This is a clear and assertive statement. At that point, you could ask a question to determine there's a legitimate reason for the employee's tardiness.

When you are making statements, certain words decrease confidence. Expressions like *kind of* and *sort of* are wishy-washy and unclear. Absolutes like *always* and *never* are dangerous to use, because nothing in human communication is ever absolute. Take the previous example: "Why do you always arrive late?" Does this employee *always* arrive late? If so, surely you would have documented the behavior and put the employee on a disciplinary action plan. *Always* and *never* are just as unclear as *kind of* and *sort of.* To communicate assertively is to communicate clearly. While it may take a lot of practice, especially when you are reacting to events, learning how to avoid these expressions can help you communicate and clarify what you're really trying to say.

To communicate assertively is to communicate clearly.

The second set of skills for improving assertiveness involves your voice. Assertive communicators recognize that emotional content is perceived as the most important part of a message. In other words, when you're speaking with someone, it is how you are delivering the message that makes the difference. Our voices have a lot to do with how a message is delivered and interpreted.

In considering how you use your voice, we're going to look at the three Ps: *pitch, power,* and *pace.* Pitch focuses on the intonation of your voice: how high or low it goes. Power focuses on the volume. Pace is the speed of your voice in combination with pauses and breaks. When you look at the three Ps, you will realize that the way you say something can drastically affect the message you are trying to convey.

Let's look at an example of a sentence emphasized in three different ways: "I *think* Mike can do this." "I think *Mike* can do this." "I think Mike *can* do this." Can you tell the difference between the three? Same words, different tone of voice, different message.

Typically, the passive tone of voice is higher-pitched, with a moderate volume, and a pace that is slower and hesitant. The aggressive voice is typically more stressed, using a higher pitch and power and usually a more rapid pace. The assertive voice is controlled in pitch, volume, and pace and is flexible and appropriate to the content.

Keys to Using Your Voice

1. Pitch
2. Power
3. Pace

Nonverbal Communication

The final skill for improving assertiveness is nonverbal communication. For your vocal clues to be relevant, there needs to be a direct and compatible correlation between what you say and what you don't say. This brings us to nonverbal or body language cues.

Nonverbal communication might be the most critical point of what you say or don't say. You can't avoid communicating with how you stand, how your face looks, your eye contact, or your proximity. These things all affect the message that you're communicating. Has someone ever said yes to you with their voice but no with their face?

Let's look at some nonverbal cues that communicate a strong message without your saying a word. Your facial expression: your smile, your frown, or your scowl. Gestures: are the gestures that you make appropriate to the message you intend, or do they seem contrived? What are you doing with your hands or arms as you speak? Could nervous habits be detracting from what you're trying to say?

Eye contact is more challenging psychologically than physically. Our eyes reveal our emotions, so sometimes it's difficult to maintain appropriate eye contact. Aim for five seconds of eye contact at a time, with brief glances away from the person or people you're addressing. Too much eye contact is intimidating, but too little makes you look as if you're hiding something.

Posture and stance: Consider how you carry yourself. Do you maintain an open posture, with your head held high and your shoulders comfortably back? Do you convey ease and confidence, or are you closed off? Do you have your arms crossed in front of you? Are your shoulders rounded?

In terms of distance or proximity, for Americans, about an arm's length is a normal distance for person-to-person communication (but beware of cultural differences). Remove barriers such as desks or tables for the most effective interpersonal communication.

Eye level relationship refers to the physical level of your eye-to-eye communication. Are you higher up than the person you're speaking with? A higher position is typically perceived as one of authority, while a level eye contact is best for mutual communication. Try to place yourself at the same physical eye level as the person you're speaking with.

What do you communicate with your physical appearance? Even if you're not in the greatest physical shape, you can still present a polished image with proper grooming and wardrobe. Consider the clothes you choose, the polish on your shoes, the cleanliness of your uniform suit or outfit. Also think about your stride. How quickly or slowly do you move about in your workplace? Do you move comfortably with a confident yet relaxed stride, or do you move quickly with tension in your body?

Finally, consider touch. A handshake is the most common form—and one of the only acceptable forms—of touch in the workplace. A handshake can create an instant perception of a person's personality or confidence level. Is your handshake firm but not overbearing, confident yet friendly?

Even without words, the body is always communicating something. Even by refusing to communicate, you are still sending messages. Nonverbal communication gives clues to sincerity, and any discrepancy of signals will diminish the impact of the words. In other words, if you're saying that you are very happy but you are frowning and your posture is closed, your messages don't match. When your words and body language are not in harmony, the recipient of your communication will always believe the tone of your voice and body language over the words you are using.

Maximizing Assertiveness

Here are a few more tips for maximizing your assertiveness.

1. **Describe; don't judge.** This comes down to describing a behavior instead of attaching a personal label. For example, use, "When I'm speaking and you interrupt me, it frustrates me" instead of "You're rude." Say, "Did you know that report is missing data?" instead of, "You're not going to turn in that report, are you?" By specifically describing the behavior at issue, your communication will be more respectful to the listener.
2. **It's OK to make a statement without explanation.** It's enough to say no. You don't have to explain why.
3. **Be persistent.** When someone keeps pushing you for a more detailed answer, instead of breaking down, just keep repeating the same answer. This is the broken-record technique. Suppose you've already said that you're only available for a meeting at 2 p.m but you're being asked to meet at 3 p.m. Simply repeat, "I can meet you at 2 p.m."
4. **Practice.** Take one thing at a time. Examine where you are currently on the assertiveness scale and think about your own personal barriers: what might they be? Start to

work through your own personalized solution. Assertive communication is a choice. It's not always the easiest choice, but in the long run, it is the one that brings lasting and high-quality results.

Key Points in This Chapter

This chapter has covered passive, aggressive, and assertive styles. It has explained why the assertive style is better than the other two. It discussed the four Rs of assertiveness as well as the ABCs of rational thinking and removing obstacles to communication. It discussed barriers in self-concept and how to eliminate them. It presented assertiveness scripts as a way of enhancing effective communication. It emphasized the extreme importance of the role of nonverbal communication, including tone of voice, posture, and personal appearance.

SIX

Conquering Procrastination

In this chapter, we'll discuss conquering procrastination to enhance mental endurance and productivity. We will focus on several areas:
1. Why do we procrastinate?
2. Conquering the common causes of procrastination.
3. The three Ps for overcoming procrastination.
4. Practicing productivity techniques.
5. Enhancing mental endurance.

Procrastination is a complex phenomenon that is influenced by various cognitive, emotional, and behavioral factors. It is the result of the interaction of various brain regions and systems.

Some research suggests that it may be related to how the brain regulates and manages tasks and goals; certain brain areas and systems, such as the prefrontal cortex and the amygdala, may play a role in this process. Other factors such as impulsivity, emotional regulation, and decision-making may also contribute to procrastination.

Ultimately, the exact causes of procrastination are not fully understood, and more research is needed to explain the underlying mechanisms. But all is not lost. This chapter will discuss a number of strategies, techniques, and tips that will help you to overcome procrastination.

Causes of Procrastination

People tend to procrastinate and lose focus in the workplace for a variety of reasons. Here are some of the most common ones:

1. **Lack of motivation or interest** in the task at hand. If you are not motivated to complete a task, you may find it difficult to start it or maintain focus and concentration while working on it. Similarly, if you perceive a task as unimportant or unengaging, you may be less likely to invest time and effort into it. When you lack motivation or interest, you may engage in other activities that are more pleasurable or rewarding, which can lead to more procrastination.
2. **Difficulty or perceived difficulty.** If you perceive a task as difficult, you may be more likely to put it off or avoid it altogether. This is because difficulty can increase feelings of anxiety and uncertainty, which may make it more challenging for you to initiate or engage in that task. When you perceive a job as difficult, you may become overwhelmed by the challenge, leading to more procrastination.

> **Common Causes of Procrastination**
>
> 1. Lack of motivation or interest
> 2. Difficulty or perceived difficulty
> 3. Lack of the necessary skills or knowledge
> 4. Distractions
> 5. Overwhelm
> 6. Poor time management
> 7. Lack of clear goals or direction
> 8. Fear

3. **Lack of the necessary skills or knowledge** to complete the task. Research suggests that when a task is difficult, it requires more cognitive resources, which may lead to mental fatigue and increased procrastination.
4. **Distractions** such as leisure activities may contribute to procrastination by providing easy and available alternatives to the task at hand. Social media in particular are designed to be engaging and enjoyable, which can make them a difficult temptation to resist. The instant gratification provided by these activities can make it hard to focus on your work, because you're battling between instant gratification and getting the work done.

    These activities can consume a lot of time and energy, which can leave you with less time and energy for your work. Sometimes it can be shocking to see reports on your smartphone of how much screen time you've had.
5. **Overwhelm,** or too many tasks on the to-do list. When you are presented with a large number of tasks, you may

find it difficult to prioritize and organize them effectively. You can even find it challenging to know where to start. This can lead to feelings of anxiety and uncertainty, causing resistance to starting or engaging in any of the tasks. This sense of overwhelm can also lead to a cycle of procrastination, whereby you keep postponing tasks till the next day, which increases the number of tasks you have to do, making you feel still more overwhelmed.

6. **Poor time management.** When you don't manage your time effectively, you may not have enough time to complete all of your tasks, leading again to stress, anxiety, and procrastination.

    Poor time management can lead to a last-minute rush to complete tasks at the last moment, often causing lower quality of work as well as stress. When you don't have a clear understanding of how much time a task will take, you may underestimate the time required, which can lead to frustration when you realize you've run out of time altogether.

    If you don't manage your time well, you might find yourself with blocks of time with nothing scheduled. You might fill it with leisure activities, social media, or other distractions, leading you to delay the task that you should be working on.

7. **A lack of clear goals or direction** can contribute to procrastination by making it difficult for you to understand the purpose or importance of a task. Without clear goals or direction, it can be hard to know what you should be working on, which can make it challenging to stay

motivated, leading back to the first common reason for procrastination: lack of motivation.

A lack of clear goals or direction can make it difficult to set priorities or measure progress, which again can reduce motivation and engagement. This can in turn lead to feelings of aimlessness and lack of direction, reinforcing the impulse toward procrastination.

Procrastination can be caused by any combination of the above factors. It can be intensified by stress, anxiety, and other mental health issues. Understanding the underlying causes of procrastination can help you find ways to overcome it.

Fear

There is one more common reason for procrastination, and it is a big one: fear. Here are five of the most common fears in the workplace that affect mental endurance:

1. **Fear of failure.** This can hold people back and prevent them from taking necessary risks or pursuing new opportunities.
2. **Fear of change.** Change can be difficult for many people. The fear of change can lead to resistance and difficulty adapting to new situations.
3. **Fear of the unknown.** The unknown can be scary, and fear of the unknown can make it difficult for people to embrace new challenges or take on new roles.
4. **Fear of conflict.** Conflict is a natural part of any workplace, but some people are afraid of confrontation or disagreement, which can reduce their mental endurance and ability to work with others.

5. **Fear of being judged.** Many people are afraid of being judged by their colleagues or supervisors, which can lead to anxiety and stress and ultimately to procrastination.

The Most Common Workplace Fears
1. Fear of failure
2. Fear of change
3. Fear of the unknown
4. Fear of conflict
5. Fear of being judged

Conquering the Causes

Now let's discover how to conquer the common causes of procrastination as well as the five most common fears in the workplace. We will first discuss the strategies at a high level and then go deeper later in the chapter.

Here are some tips:
- Develop a clear understanding of what you want to accomplish.
- Set specific measurable goals to work towards.
- Break down complex tasks into smaller, manageable chunks.
- Once you've broken down your tasks, prioritize them based on importance and urgency, and set a deadline for each step.
- Use time management techniques to plan your day, your week, and month in advance.

- Use a calendar or to-do list to help you stay on track and manage your time.
- Identify and eliminate sources of distraction such as social media or other leisure activities that are preventing you from focusing on your work. This could include turning off your phone, closing unnecessary tabs on your computer, or finding a quiet place to work.
- Reward yourself for completing tasks with small treats or breaks. This will keep you motivated and will make it easier for you to focus.

Overcoming Fears

Now let's learn how to overcome the five common fears that affect mental endurance and productivity.

Fear of failure.

When you set unrealistic or overly ambitious goals, you set yourself up for failure. Setting realistic goals increases the likelihood of success, which can help build confidence and reduce the fear of failure. There is an inverse relation between confidence and the fear of failure: confidence works to eliminate the fear of failure.

Large tasks can be overwhelming. To mitigate this difficulty, break down large tasks or large projects into smaller, more manageable steps. This will make the tasks seem less daunting and increase the chance of success.

Recognize and celebrate small successes, which can help you build momentum and maintain a positive attitude, increasing motivation to continue trying.

Failure can be seen as a gift: it can provide valuable feedback. When you do fail, try to understand what went wrong and what you could have done differently. How can you avoid similar mistakes in the future?

> **Failure can be seen as a gift: it can provide valuable feedback.**

Fear of change.

Change, especially if it's a big one, can be overwhelming, but it can bring new opportunities and positive outcomes. Focus on the potential benefits. To make the change less daunting, again, try breaking your new tasks down into smaller and more manageable steps.

One of the best ways to overcome the fear of change is to take action. Start small, but take a first step in the direction of the change. It will help you to build momentum.

Fear of the unknown.

This often stems from a lack of information. Gather as much information as possible about the situation. This can reduce uncertainty and increase your sense of control. The unknown can be overwhelming, but remember that you can't control everything. The unknown is a part of life, and you can't always control what happens. Identify what you *can* control and focus on taking action there. Try to embrace uncertainty and see it as an opportunity for growth and learning.

The unknown can be intimidating. Taking small steps towards it can build momentum and make it seem less daunting. It's about seeing the opportunities and possibilities in the unknown rather than the negatives.

Fear of conflict.

As we've already seen, one key to resolving conflict is effective communication. Active listening involves paying close attention to what the other person is saying without interrupting or getting defensive. This can diminish misunderstanding and build trust. It can be easy to become entrenched in your own point of view, but trying to understand where the other person is coming from can reduce conflict.

In *The Seven Habits of the Highly Effective People*, Stephen R. Covey lists the fifth habit as seeking to understand versus being understood. Put the priority on understanding the other person rather than getting them to understand you. Moreover, as we saw in the last chapter, assertive communication involves expressing your thoughts and feelings in a clear and direct way without being either aggressive or passive. This can reduce the likelihood of misunderstandings and can set clear boundaries.

If you have contributed to the conflict, take responsibility for your actions. If an apology is necessary, give one. This can diffuse a tense situation and move it towards resolution.

Finally, conflicts often arise when people have different needs or wants. Compromise can help to find a middle ground and reach a resolution that satisfies both parties. You're looking for areas that you have in common. If you can find commonality in what both of you want and why you want it, there's an opportunity for compromise.

Fear of being judged.

The fear of being judged is becoming more and more of an issue in our social media age. Many people are afraid of being judged by their colleagues or supervisors, which can lead to anxiety and stress, and ultimately to procrastination. Ultimately, the fear of being judged arises from a combination of the four fears we have already discussed. We fear conflict with our colleagues, the unknown of how our actions will be perceived, the fear that changes we make will leave us worse off in the eyes of our colleagues, which all ultimately leads to our fear that we will fail in our role. The remedy for this fear is to apply the strategies we have already discussed with the previous four fears.

Three Final Strategies

There are three final strategies for conquering the common causes of procrastination and the five most common fears.

1. **Embrace a growth mindset.** People with a growth mindset believe that they can develop their abilities through effort and learning. Embracing this mentality can enable you to view failure as an opportunity to learn and grow rather than as a setback. It can also help you view change as an opportunity to learn and grow rather than as a threat.

    A growth mindset can also help you implement the strategies and techniques you are learning in this chap-

> **Strategies for Conquering Procrastination**
> 1. Embrace a growth mindset.
> 2. Practice mindfulness.
> 3. Seek support.

ter to conquer procrastination once and for all. If you want to learn more about the growth mindset, you can check out the book *Mindset: The New Psychology of Success* by Carol S. Dweck.

2. **Practice mindfulness.** Mindfulness can help you stay present and focused in the moment rather than getting caught up in worries about the future or what others may be thinking. Techniques like meditation and deep breathing can help you manage stress and anxiety associated with the fear of change and the unknown.

   Focusing on the present moment will help you be more engaged and less self-conscious. These techniques can also aid you in managing your emotions amid conflict, enabling you to remain calm and rational. Mindfulness can be useful in acquiring a growth mindset and reframing how you view failure.

3. **Seek support.** Surround yourself with supportive people who encourage you to take risks and celebrate your successes. You can also seek guidance from a therapist or counselor to work through underlying issues that may be contributing to your fears and to develop coping strategies.

It's important to have a support system in place. Seek out the support of friends and family who can provide guidance and encouragement when you're facing the fear of change.

Prepare, Prioritize, and Plan

Now let's discover the three Ps for overcoming procrastination once and for all. (These aren't the same as the three Ps for voice control, which we've already explored.)

> **Three Ps for Overcoming Procrastination**
> 1. Preparation
> 2. Prioritization
> 3. Planning

Preparation

Let's start with *preparation*. This important strategy for overcoming procrastination reduces the feeling of being overwhelmed and makes it easier to start working.

Here are some ways to implement this strategy.

Break tasks into smaller, manageable chunks. Keep breaking down larger projects until you are left with manageable steps. It may take several layers to get to those manageable steps.

Gather necessary materials ahead of time. Have all the materials you need before starting a task, including books, notes, equipment, and supplies. Having everything you need on hand will prevent delays and interruptions.

Identify and eliminate distractions. As we've already observed, this could include turning off your phone, closing unnecessary tabs on your computer, or finding a quiet place to work.

Prioritization

The second P is *prioritize*. Prioritizing is an important strategy, because it helps ensure that important deadlines are met and prevents last-minute scrambling.

Priorities are the things that are most important to you. Daily goals are the specific tasks or objectives that you aim to accomplish in a day. Priorities may be long-term goals or values that you're working towards, such as getting a promotion at work, saving money, or maintaining good relationships.

Daily goals, on the other hand, involve specific steps that you take each day to move closer to achieving your priorities. One daily goal might be to spend thirty minutes working on a project for a promotion, or to make a budget and stick to it. By setting and focusing on daily goals that align with your priorities, you can make progress towards achieving what is most important to you. Here are some ways to implement this strategy.

Prioritize based on importance and deadline. Determine which tasks are most important and need to be completed first. Take deadlines into account in order to focus on the most critical tasks first and ensure that you meet important deadlines.

Prioritize based on importance and deadline.

A *critical* task is one that is important or necessary for the success of a project or goal. It is usually time-sensitive. Critical tasks often require a higher level of skill or expertise as well as additional time and resources to complete.

On the other hand, a *random* task is one that is not necessarily important or necessary for a project's success. It may be less time-sensitive and may have no direct impact on the outcome. Random tasks are usually less urgent and require less skill or expertise to complete.

Prioritize critical tasks, and make sure that you have completed them in a timely manner, while making time for random tasks as needed.

Use a prioritization matrix: a tool that helps you prioritize tasks based on their importance and urgency. By placing tasks in different quadrants, you can see which tasks need to be done first and which can be put off until later. There are different variations of these prioritization matrices, but a common one is the Eisenhower Matrix, so called because it was supposedly invented by the late president Dwight D. Eisenhower. It separates tasks into four categories, as follows:

The Eisenhower Matrix

	Urgent	Not urgent
Important		
Not important		

Let's review those four categories.

Urgent and important.
These tasks need to be done immediately and are of high importance. They should be done first, as they have a high impact and a short deadline.

Important but not urgent.
These tasks are important but not pressing. Even so, they should be scheduled and completed as soon as possible, because they will have a high impact on your goals and objectives.

Urgent but not important.
These tasks are urgent but do not have a high level of importance. They should be evaluated and delegated or outsourced if possible.

Not urgent and not important.
These tasks can be put off until later or possibly eliminated.

To use a prioritization matrix, write down all of your tasks in a list first. Evaluate each task based on their level of importance and urgency. Place each task in the appropriate quadrant. Start working on the tasks in the urgent and important quadrant first, then move on to those that are important but not urgent, then urgent and not important. Review your progress and adjust your prioritization as needed.

The Eisenhower Matrix is a useful tool for identifying and prioritizing tasks, but it's not a one-size-fits-all solution. It is simply a guide. Review and adjust your priorities as you progress. Keep the context of each task in mind and adapt the matrix accordingly.

Critical tasks typically fall into the category of urgent and important: they are both necessary and time-sensitive. They may also require a higher skill level. We tend to gravitate to simpler quick wins by completing random tasks, because it feels good to check things off the list.

Here are some suggestions to find a balance between the critical and the random tasks.

1. **Prioritize tasks.** Use a tool like the matrix above and ensure that critical tasks are given the highest priority.
2. **Use a task management system** such as Trello or Asana. It can help you organize your tasks and keep track of them, making it easier to see what needs to be done and when. You may have this type of system included in your calendar.
3. **Set aside dedicated blocks of time** for critical tasks. This will help you focus and get them done more efficiently.
4. **Take breaks.** Taking breaks and giving yourself time to recharge will enable you to stay focused and prevent burnout.
5. **Seek help when needed.** Don't be afraid to ask for help in completing tasks. It's better to do that than to struggle on your own and risk missing deadlines or making mistakes. Always choose seeking help instead of when you feel that failure may be inevitable.
6. **Eliminate low-priority tasks.** Once you've identified tasks that are not important or that can be put off, consider eliminating them, or delegate them if possible. This will free up time and energy for more important tasks.

> **Balancing Critical and Random Tasks**
> 1. Prioritize tasks.
> 2. Use a task management system.
> 3. Set aside dedicated blocks of time.
> 4. Take breaks.
> 5. Seek help.
> 6. Eliminate low-priority tasks.

Planning

The third and final P is *planning*. This keeps you focused and on track and makes it easier to see how much progress you're making. Here are some ways to implement this strategy.

Plan in advance by creating a schedule or a to-do list. It's best to plan out the entire week. Don't leave it on a day-to-day process. This will help to keep you on track and will make it easier to see how much progress you are making. A best practice at the end of the day is to look back and celebrate your accomplishments.

Set specific, measurable goals for each task and use them to guide your planning. This will enable you to focus on the most important aspects of the task and to ensure that you are making progress.

Schedule your tasks into your plan after you've broken them down into manageable sections. This will make it easier to focus on one step at a time and see progress on bigger projects and tasks.

Use a calendar to schedule in your time for tasks and deadlines, so you can stay on track and avoid last minute scrambling.

Be flexible. Be prepared to adjust or revise your plans as necessary: life happens and things change. Be open to revising your plan if it is needed.

By using the strategies above, you can stay focused and on track, and you will easily see how much progress you are making.

Designing an Efficient Workspace

Here are some general tips for designing an efficient workspace. Consider how you work best and what you need in your workspace to support that. For example, do you need a quiet space to concentrate, or do you prefer a more collaborative environment?

Consider the size and layout of your workspace and how you can use it most effectively. Think about factors such as lighting, temperature, and comfort. Keep the tools and supplies you use most often within easy reach. Use storage solutions such as bins, shelfs, and drawers to keep things organized and out of sight. Add personal touches to make your workspace feel more comfortable and inviting. These can include items such as plants, pictures, and decorations.

Make sure your workspace is set up in a way that promotes good posture and prevents physical strain. Good practices include using an ergonomic chair and placing your computer monitor at eye level. Many people have found standing desks to be very comfortable as well as more efficient.

Productivity: The Fourth P

Now let's consider how you can practice productivity—a fourth P—with three powerful techniques. They are methods and strategies that help you manage your time, work more efficiently and effectively, and improve overall productivity.

These techniques can include time management methods such as the Pomodoro technique, which breaks work into focused intervals separated by short breaks, as well as methods for aligning work with your natural energy levels, such as ultradian work rhythms.

Productivity techniques are designed to help you achieve more in less time, reduce stress and burnout, and improve well-being. These techniques can be adapted to fit individual needs and used in both personal and professional settings.

Productivity techniques offer several benefits. By breaking work into shorter intervals and aligning your work schedule with your natural energy levels, you can stay more focused and avoid distractions. These techniques can help you prioritize your tasks and use your time more efficiently.

By managing your workload and avoiding overworking, you can reduce stress and the risk of burnout. By working more efficiently and effectively, you can get more done in less time. Managing your time effectively, you can make more time for other activities and improve your work-life balance.

Tools like DeskTime can help you identify your work patterns and habits, so you can understand where you may be wasting time and how to improve your efficiency.

Different techniques may work better for different people, so find the one that fits you the best and adjust it for your specific needs.

The Pomodoro Technique

The Pomodoro technique is a time management method developed by Francesco Cirillo in the late 1980s. It is based on the idea that frequent breaks can improve mental agility and that breaking work into shorter, more focused intervals can help you stay on task and avoid burnout. The method is named after the tomato-shaped kitchen timer that Cirillo used when he first developed the technique.

The basic structure of the Pomodoro technique is as follows: Decide on the task you want to accomplish. Set a timer for twenty-five minutes. This is considered one Pomodoro. Work on the task until the timer rings. Take a short break. Five minutes is recommended. Repeat steps one through four for four Pomodoros, then take a longer break: fifteen to thirty minutes.

The Pomodoro technique is highly adaptable, and you can adjust the time intervals to fit your needs. It's common to use shorter Pomodoros when working on difficult tasks and longer Pomodoros when working on more straightforward tasks.

One key element of the Pomodoro technique is the use of a timer. This helps you to stay focused on the task at hand and avoid distractions. When the timer rings, it reminds you to take a break and recharge. The Pomodoro technique is not a one-size-fits-all solution, and it may take some experimentation to find the time intervals that work best for you, but overall, it is a simple and effective way to boost your productivity and manage your time.

DeskTime

DeskTime is a productivity-tracking software that allows you to monitor your work habits and identify areas for improvement. The software runs in the back of your computer and automatically records the apps and websites you use as well as the duration of your breaks, providing detailed reports on your work patterns. The Productivity Pulse feature displays your productivity levels in real time, allowing you to see how you're doing throughout the day. Reports and Analytics give you insight into your work habits, including how much time you spend on different tasks, when you're the most productive, and which apps and websites you use most. Integrations with other productivity tools such as calendars and to-do lists provide a holistic view of your work habits. The team management feature tracks the productivity of your team members and helps you implement a more organized workflow.

DeskTime is a powerful tool. By tracking your time and providing detailed reports, it can identify areas where you're wasting time. It offers a range of features to help you stay focused and avoid distractions.

Ultradian Work Rhythms

Ultradian work rhythms are the natural fluctuations in energy and focus that occur throughout the day. These rhythms can last anywhere from ninety minutes to several hours and can affect your productivity. Understanding your ultradian rhythms can help you plan your workday around your natural energy levels.

There are a few different ways to determine your ultradian work rhythm. Pay attention to your energy levels throughout the day. Notice when you feel the most alert and focused and when you start to feel tired or restless. These natural fluctuations can give you a sense of your rhythms. Try working for ninety minutes, then take a twenty- to thirty-minute break. See how you feel after each session and adjust your schedule accordingly. Keep track of your energy levels and work habits over a period of several days or even several weeks in order to identify patterns and understand your rhythms. DeskTime can help you track your work patterns and identify your rhythms.

Everyone's rhythms are different, and they can change over time. The best way to discover your own rhythms is to pay attention to your body and experiment with different work schedules. A best practice would be to check in with your rhythms and patterns once every three to six months to notice any changes and make the necessary adjustments.

> The best way to discover your own rhythms is to pay attention to your body and experiment with different work schedules.

Enhancing Endurance

Let's now discuss how you can remain persistent in implementing these strategies and techniques.

To be persistent means to continue doing something despite obstacles or difficulties. It is the ability to persevere and not give up easily. By recognizing and addressing bad habits, eliminating distractions, and practicing self-care, you can minimize procrastination and enhance mental endurance.

Here are a few strategies that can help you spot and stop bad coping habits.

1. **Identify the root cause.** Are you feeling overwhelmed by your workload? Are you struggling with low motivation or low energy? Once you have a better understanding of the root cause, you can develop strategies to address it.
2. As we've already seen, **setting clear, achievable goals** can help you stay focused and motivated. A clear sense of what you are working towards can make it easier to avoid getting sidetracked.
3. A **structured schedule** can also enable you to stay organized and on track. This might involve setting aside specific times, not just for work, but also for breaks and leisure activities.
4. **Take breaks to rest and recharge.** Instead of relying on bad coping habits to deal with stress or boredom, try taking a walk, stretching, or engaging in a relaxing activity, like meditation or yoga.

Eliminating Distractions

Another strategy for remaining persistent is to eliminate distractions. Although we've already discussed this subject, let's dig a little deeper for specific tips.

Determine what types of interruptions are acceptable and when, and communicate these boundaries to your colleagues. If possible, create a separate workspace where you can focus on your work without interruptions. If you work in a noisy environment, consider using noise canceling headphones to block out distractions. When you need to focus on a specific task, turn off notifications on your computer and phone.

A more radical step is to remove Facebook from your phone. If you can keep it off for some weeks or even months, you can break your addiction to checking Facebook 24/7.

The Pomodoro technique can help you stay on track and avoid getting distracted by other tasks. Again, it's important to take breaks to rest your mind and recharge. Taking regular breaks throughout the day can prevent burnout. During breaks, step away from your workspace and do something that helps you relax, such as going for a walk or stretching. Whether you're working at home or you're going to a physical office, stepping away from your workspace is essential.

The final strategy for remaining persistent is self-care. Several self-care techniques can help with minimizing procrastination, staying focused, and maintaining mental endurance and productivity. Mindfulness meditation can improve focus, concentration, and reduce stress. Regular exercise or yoga and eating healthy can enhance focus, concentration, and overall well-being. Getting enough sleep is essential for maintaining mental and physical well-being. A best practice is getting seven to nine hours of sleep per night. Relaxation techniques such as deep breathing, progressive muscle relaxation, and guided imagery can reduce stress and improve focus.

We have already seen the value of time management strategies such as setting deadlines for your task and breaking it into smaller chunks. To repeat another point: seek help. If you are struggling to overcome bad coping habits, seek support from friends, family, or a mental health professional. They can provide you with the encouragement and accountability you need to make positive changes. If distractions at work are making it difficult to stay focused, consider speaking to your manager or human resources representative for additional support.

Key Points in This Chapter

Procrastination and mental fatigue are common obstacles that can impede your productivity and well-being. By recognizing and addressing bad habits, eliminating distractions, and practicing self-care, you can minimize procrastination and enhance mental endurance. Spotting and stopping bad habits, such as procrastination or multitasking, and eliminating distractions will improve your ability to focus on the task at hand and persist towards your goals.

Prioritize self-care activities to maintain a healthy work-life balance. Techniques such as mindfulness, yoga and exercise, getting enough sleep, eating a healthy diet, regular breaks, and relaxation techniques can maintain your mental and physical well-being. Remember to seek help if you find it hard to overcome procrastination.

By implementing these strategies, you can improve your ability to focus, minimize procrastination, and enhance your mental endurance.

SEVEN

Strategic Problem-Solving

The goal of this chapter is to help you improve your analytical ability, guide critical thinking, and provide practical and effective strategies for solving problems and making decisions that have lasting outcomes.

We will begin this chapter with the subject of making a decision versus strategically solving a problem. We'll proceed to the six habits of strategic thinkers and to recognizing your thinking and problem-solving style. We'll go on to cover tools for strategic problem-solving, such as the SWOT analysis and the seven-step approach to strategic problem-solving. Finally, we'll wrap up with applying this material and overcoming common obstacles.

Decisions versus Problem-Solving

Let's set the stage by distinguishing between a quick fix decision and a holistic, ongoing practice of strategic problem-solving. In this section, you'll learn how to move beyond surface level choices and drive long-term solutions that can truly access the root cause of an issue.

Let's look at the difference between making a decision and strategic problem-solving, because they really are two different things, even though they are closely related.

Decision-making is a reactive process that is focused on immediate solutions. Typically, it addresses a single problem. It will rely on available data and past experience to come up with a final decision.

> Decision-making is a reactive process that is focused on immediate solutions.

Strategic problem-solving takes a more comprehensive approach. It analyzes patterns and underlying factors, incorporating multiple stakeholders' perspectives and considering future implications. Hence it is more comprehensive.

An example of decision-making might be choosing a vendor based on current prices. An example of strategic problem-

---

Five Benefits of Strategic Problem-Solving

1. Future-proofing
2. Enhanced collaboration
3. Encouraging innovative thinking and creativity
4. Minimizing risks
5. Eliminating guesswork

solving would be developing a sustainable supply chain strategy, which requires a deeper analysis of the system and long-term considerations.

The choice between these two approaches will depend on the nature of the problem at hand and the desired outcome.

Let's proceed to look at five benefits of strategic problem-solving.

1. **Future-proofing.** Strategic problem-solving, equipped with a broader perspective on potential outcomes, allows you to anticipate and prepare for shifts in market dynamics, technology, or consumer behavior. By regularly scanning the environment and evaluating multiple scenarios, you can reduce last-minute scrambling, strengthen your organization's resilience, and make informed choices that stand the test of time.
2. **Enhanced collaboration.** As we've discussed in previous chapters, increasing collaboration and energy among diverse teams is extremely important. A strategic approach naturally invites input from various stakeholders, tapping into different skill sets and expertise to create holistic solutions. This inclusive culture not only boosts morale but also leverages the power of shared insight. It leads to richer problem-solving and a greater sense of collective ownership over outcomes.
3. **Encouraging innovative thinking and creativity.** Stepping back from day-to-day tactics to address problems from a strategic viewpoint allows room for out-of-the-box thinking. Teams are encouraged to question assumptions, explore unconventional paths, and experiment with new

methods. This approach can drive breakthroughs and spark a constant flow of fresh ideas.
4. **Minimizing risks through forward-looking analysis.** Data-driven forecasting and a rigorous exploration of potential risks help you to proactively address vulnerabilities rather than reacting to them as they arrive. By modeling different scenarios and weighing possible outcomes, you build contingency plans that protect your organization from unforeseen setbacks and ensure smoother execution of initiatives.
5. **Eliminating guesswork.** Decisions guided by structured, well-considered insight instead of hunches or short-term fixes can protect valuable time and resources. Clarity about objectives and processes helps teams focus on what matters most, allowing for more efficient workflows and faster implementation of effective solutions.

The Six Key Habits of Strategic Thinkers

By embodying these six key habits, you'll build the mindset needed for sustainable success in virtually any environment.

1. **Proactive learning.** Proactive learning involves continually expanding your knowledge by seeking out new information, insights, and perspectives before a challenge or decision point even arrives.

    A key point in proactive learning is to embrace curiosity. When you do so, you will treat each day as an opportunity to discover ideas that may inform future solutions. Being well informed helps you anticipate changes in your industry or your role in your organization.

> **Six Habits of Strategic Thinkers**
> 1. Proactive learning
> 2. Long-term vision
> 3. Flexibility
> 4. Evidence-based decision-making
> 5. A collaborative approach
> 6. Reflective analysis

You also want to foster agility. The more knowledge you have, the faster you can pivot and respond to evolving demand. In addition, cultivate innovation. Exposure to diverse viewpoints often leads to unique connections and sparks important creative insights.

Proactive learning involves regular information intake. Subscribe to industry newsletters and follow credible thought leaders on social media. Curate a personal learning playlist of podcast videos and audios that you can consume on a weekly basis.

You also want to have some sort of structured learning program: attending workshops and webinars; taking courses; or taking part in a Master Mind group, which will help you in the exchange of knowledge, ideas, and experiences.

It's also valuable to balance between breadth and depth in your proactive learning. It might be beneficial to learn a bit about many different topics in order to spot emerging patterns. Then dive deep into a particular niche or skill to become a credible subject matter expert.

2. **Long-term vision.** Long-term vision can be defined as keeping tomorrow's impact in mind when addressing today's challenges. In order to do that, you need a forward-focused mindset. Instead of only solving immediate issues, you want to align actions with long-term objectives. This strategic alignment ensures that short-term decisions will contribute to larger goals.

> Long-term vision can be defined as keeping tomorrow's impact in mind when addressing today's challenges.

Resilience is also very important: it helps organizations and individuals adapt to future market changes, technology shifts, or evolving customer needs in order to maintain a competitive edge. Being ahead of industry trends can help you launch new products or services faster than your competitors.

One strategy for fostering long-term vision is scenario planning. Outline multiple possible future outcomes, such as best-case and worst-case scenarios, and identify key triggers that might accelerate or hinder each scenario.

Have vision-driven goals. Set clear, measurable long-term goals, and check short-term tasks for alignment with them. Use OKRs—which stands for *objectives and key results*—or other goal-setting frameworks. Early trendspotting is also helpful. Monitor emerging technology, demographics, and economic indicators for early signals of change. Adjust strategic priorities based on these observed patterns or shifts.

3. **Flexibility.** Flexibility is the willingness to revise assumptions and adapt to new data. Adapt; don't react. Agility in thinking and planning prevents stagnation and keeps you open to better, more innovative solutions. In a dynamic market, the ability to pivot quickly can be a lifeline.

You also want to prevent tunnel vision. Sticking too rigidly to an original plan can stifle creativity or lead to missed opportunities. As we've already seen in more than one context, employee engagement is also very important. Teams feel more valued when their feedback or discoveries lead to tangible shifts in strategy. Since they know they're contributing, they are more engaged.

How do you stay flexible? Check in regularly with your team. Schedule periodic reviews to assess whether assumptions made early in the planning process still hold true. Encourage open dialogue about emerging insights or obstacles. Have a plan B and a plan C along with plan A in place to mitigate potential surprises. Moreover, you want to assign roles and responsibility for implementing alternative plans as well, so you know who's accountable for what.

For some people, flexibility will require a mindset shift. You have to be constantly thinking about building and cultivating a growth mindset in your organization. Make sure to celebrate learning from mistakes. Reward teams and/or individuals who identify when an existing plan needs to be adapted.

4. **Evidence-based decision-making.** This is using data, past outcomes, and logical reasoning to inform your decisions and solutions. It's a matter of balancing intuition

and facts. While intuition can play a big role in decisions, even strategic ones, evidence ensures that those decisions rest on a solid, objective foundation. Having data to back your decision can highlight potential pitfalls early and reduce your risks.

Transparency is always important. Clear metrics and documentation make it easier to justify decisions. Continuous improvement is key as well. Reviewing outcomes systematically reveals what works and what doesn't and provides the evidence to show why.

How do you gather and use this evidence? Identify relative metrics like KPIs (key performance indicators). Gather reliable data sources through surveys, CRM (customer relationship management) systems, or market research. Make sure that the data is accurate, up-to-date, and—which is very important—ethically sourced.

You also want to have good analysis techniques. Maybe you use tools like trend analysis, statistical modeling, or an AB testing process to interpret the data. (AB testing involves randomly showing different versions—A and B—to users and then analyzing which version leads to more conversions, clicks, or other desired outcomes.)

Consider both quantitative and qualitative insights for a more complete picture. You can use decision-making frameworks, possibly a structured method like PDCA, which stands for *plan, do, check,* and *act*. You could also use a cost-benefit analysis template.

You also want to keep track of your assumptions, especially if you don't have hard facts to back them up. If you make an assumption based on data, revisit that evi-

> **PDCA for Decision-Making**
> 1. Plan
> 2. Do
> 3. Check
> 4. Act

dence periodically to make sure that it is still valid and see if anything new has emerged.

5. **A collaborative approach.** The collaborative approach involves listening to and leveraging diverse viewpoints to enhance creativity.

   One key is the power of diversity. Multidisciplinary teams can spark breakthroughs by combining varied experiences, skills, and cultural perspectives. Multiple perspectives illuminate blind spots and generate richer ideas from a variety of experiences and thought processes. Diversity improves buy-in as well: key members feel more motivated when their input is valued. Furthermore, diversity leads to faster problem-solving: because everyone contributes, you have more collective knowledge to tackle challenges.

   How can you have a more collaborative approach? You can hold an inclusive brainstorming session. Encourage every voice to be heard, and set ground rules that promote respect and openness. For cross-functional collaboration, create project groups that bring in different departments or skill sets. These can break down silos that often close us off and keep us in tunnel vision.

In addition, be sure to use active listening and open feedback techniques. Employ paraphrasing and follow-up questions to fully understand others' perspectives.

6. **Reflective analysis.** Reflective analysis is the process of regularly examining your outcomes, biases, and assumptions, both individually and at the team or organizational level. This process ensures that both successes and failures become stepping stones to growth. It will also help identify blind spots and recurring patterns that may be hindering your progress.

   To employ a reflective analysis, have regular debriefs. After each project or milestone, discuss what went well and what needs improvement. Critique processes, not people, and remain solution-focused.

   A root cause analysis is valuable when something has failed. Look beyond symptoms to identify systemic or underlying issues.

   Sometimes we go to the doctor, and all the doctor knows to do is treat the symptoms, because they don't know the root cause of an issue. While that sometimes may be true in a business situation, usually you can get to the root causes. Don't be satisfied with treating the symptom.

   It's best to employ all of these six habits as a collective rather than an individual trying to do them. Working as a collective, you'll find that strategies are better, decisions are better, and outcomes are definitely improved.

Recognizing your Thinking Style

Now we will focus on understanding how your personal style shapes your approach to challenges. By recognizing the strengths and limitations of your natural style, you can consciously adapt your methods. You can develop more strategic ways of thinking and create better approaches to complex issues.

An individual's problem-solving style influences how they interpret information, prioritize tasks, and arrive at solutions. Some people rely heavily on data and logic, while others lean on gut intuition. Neither approach is necessarily right or wrong on its own, but they do have pros and cons. By understanding these different tendencies, teams can combine strengths to generate a more balanced problem-solving process.

Recognizing your unique style also helps you adapt more effectively to diverse work environments, foster better collaboration, and consciously address any blind spots that might limit your personal effectiveness and impact the entire team.

The first style is the *analytical* style, which focuses on data, logic, and detail. This style excels at dissecting complex information and identifying patterns or root causes. Individuals of this type are thorough and accurate and spend much time gathering and interpreting data. They can detect inconsistencies or potential pitfalls in a proposed plan.

The analytical style has its cons as well. This type of person might risk analysis paralysis: delaying decisions while researching for more and more data, so that the research never ends. This individual might struggle to make quick

> **Problem-Solving Styles**
> 1. Analytical
> 2. Intuitive
> 3. Strategic
> 4. Directive

decisions in ambiguous situations, where complete information isn't available.

The analytical individual is good at dealing with large data sets and precision tasks, such as budgeting, analytics, and quality control. They're good at conducting risk assessments and verifying the feasibility of a particular solution.

Next is the *intuitive* style. This person relies on instinct, pattern recognition, and learned experience, often synthesizing information quickly and without explicit step-by-step analysis.

This style does have a lot of strengths. They often shine at swift decision-making in a fast-paced or novel situation. They also provide creative sparks that come from making connections others may miss. They're great at brainstorming sessions that require imaginative or unconventional ideas.

Intuitive types have drawbacks. They may overlook important data or inconsistencies in the rush to follow a gut feeling. They can struggle to explain decisions to more data-driven colleagues.

The third thinking style is the *strategic* style. This style balances creative thinking with evidence-based reasoning. These individuals are in the middle between the analytical and intuitive types. They keep a long-term view in mind, so they're continually scanning the horizon for future trends and big-picture implications. They also combine analytical depth with flexible thinking to drive innovative yet practical solutions.

Strategic types have their pitfalls as well. They may invest too much time in forecasting and planning, possibly missing short-term big wins. They also risk being perceived as less action-oriented if their strategies remain high-level without a clear execution plan.

The strategic thinker is best used for shaping organizational vision or setting long-term goals. They're also good at coordinating cross-functional initiatives that require both creative insight and data-driven validation.

The last thinking style is the *directive*. The directive type is quick and decisive in approach. They often leverage authority and past experiences to make calls.

Strengths of this style include efficiency at high-stakes or emergency situations, where time is limited. They also provide clear leadership, direction, and momentum to a team. But their very capacity for making a call may lead them to overlook input from others. That could stifle collaboration, in addition to missing the valuable insights of others. They may also be apt to dismiss new data that don't align with their own preconceived plan.

The best use for the directive type is in turnaround situations, where quick, prompt decisions must be made. They're also great at leading a team that needs clear and direct guidance to stay on task.

These are the four common thinking styles. Maybe you've been able to identify the one to which you think you're most inclined. Even so, you have the capacity to use all of these styles in certain circumstances. The point is not to label yourself as merely, say, an analytical thinker, but, if you have that tendency, it's likely that when push comes to shove, that style will come to the fore.

Challenging Your Style

Let's look at three tips for challenging your own style.

1. **Encourage open dialogue.** Foster an environment where every team member feels comfortable sharing their ideas and voicing their concerns. You may want to hold structured brainstorming sessions, in which no idea is labeled as a bad idea. Let everybody feel safe to contribute.

    Why does this matter? Individually, it exposes you to different viewpoints that you might not have considered. For the group, it encourages richer, more creative solutions. You definitely don't want everybody to think the same way all the time, because then creativity goes out the window.

2. **Step into others' perspectives.** You've heard the expression "walk a mile in someone else's shoes." Think a mile in their brain. Ask the what-if and the why not to spark exploration of alternatives. Use role-playing or scenario mapping to see an issue through someone else's eyes: maybe it's a customer, maybe it's a colleague, maybe it's a stakeholder. The benefits are considerable. This exercise will expand your empathy and identify blind spots that you might have toward other styles. It will also

> **How to Challenge Styles**
> 1. Encourage open dialogue.
> 2. Step into others' perspectives.
> 3. Embrace feedback.

strengthen collaboration by showing that you value and understand—or at least try to understand—others' viewpoints.

3. **Embrace feedback.** We've already encountered this suggestion in other contexts. View feedback as an opportunity to learn rather than as a personal critique (this requires effort for some people). Don't take everything as an attack. Focus on the actionable elements of the feedback. Think about what you can do differently or better next time.

In practical application, schedule periodic feedback sessions with peers or mentors, and keep track of repeated patterns to spot areas that need improvement. Embracing feedback promotes continual growth and adaptation and refines thinking style, shedding light on strengths and weaknesses.

Practice Self-Awareness

What are your next steps? Certainly you want to know your thinking style. Awareness of your default approach is crucial. Be willing to explore and promote your own ability to adapt and integrate.

In diverse teams, leverage the strengths of each style, whether it's analytical precision, intuitive leading, strategic foresight, or directive clarity. Take advantage of the best of all those worlds.

Challenge and grow regularly. Question your own beliefs about the decision or project at hand. Doing so will keep you flexible and enable you to move with the team instead of against it. You'll be open to fresh perspectives and ready to grow.

Combining awareness of these thinking styles is an ongoing self-challenge. But it will enable you to cultivate a mindset that is more agile, collaborative, and effective at solving problems in today's dynamic environment.

Tools for Strategic Problem-Solving

In chapter 2, we encountered the SWOT analysis for forward-thinking strategy. To refresh your memory, SWOT stands for *strengths, weaknesses, opportunities,* and *threats.*

As you do a SWOT analysis, you can begin by looking at the *strengths* in this forward-thinking strategy. Ask, what are the *weaknesses* of the situation, or maybe ourselves personally? Where are the *opportunities* that we can take advantage of? What are the *threats* to this process? When you are able to assess internal capabilities as well evolving external conditions, you'll be ready for those eventualities.

For ongoing strategic direction, use the SWOT analysis as a kind of checkup. In a medical checkup, we get our blood pressure taken and our reflexes checked. Similarly, with your SWOT analysis, you want to align your insights with your long-term goal.

Leverage strengths by linking your identified strengths to larger strategic objectives, such as expanding into a new market or enhancing a product line.

Address weaknesses. For your team, create action plans like upskilling or investing in technology to reduce internal vulnerabilities and maintain competitiveness.

You want to seize opportunities as well. Integrate market openings or emerging trends into your roadmap so that you can allocate resources effectively to explore or invest in these areas.

Next, you want to mitigate threats. Develop a contingency plan for what-if scenarios. For example, if a new competitor enters your market, how are you going to pivot? How will your team adapt and shift in response? Consider multiple scenarios: best-case, worst-case, and most likely. Do that for each opportunity or threat. Create strategies for each scenario to remain agile and keep from being caught off guard by any sudden shift.

Incorporate SWOT into your daily decision-making. The SWOT analysis should be a living document, so you'll want to refer to it when evaluating new projects or initiatives. Does the project leverage core strengths or address a weakness? Use it to track how you're progressing with improvements or proactive measures against possible threats.

Incorporate SWOT into your daily decision-making.

Finally, schedule regular touchpoints to review progress and provide support. During these sessions, use your SWOT to ensure that your progress is genuine, aligning with your overall initiatives, goal, and vision.

Scenario Planning

Let's look at a case study. Here is the scenario: A midsize tech company is evaluating the launch of a new software product. They do a SWOT analysis, and they determine that they have the strengths of existing expertise in software development, solid brand reputation, and a loyal customer base. They also note some weaknesses: limited marketing reach and outdated backend systems that need upgrading. In opportunities, they notice that there is a growing demand for remote collaboration tools. They may also be able to partner with cloud service providers. Threats include future obsolescence of their product.

The company will use its strengths. They will utilize brand credibility to gain early adopters. They're going to act on their weaknesss as well. They will also invest in marketing and infrastructure so that they can scale effectively. The action that they take on their opportunity would be to develop integration features: the popular cloud platform. As far as threats are concerned, they're looking to budget for regular product updates and spend money on research and development in order to stay ahead of the game.

The Seven-Step Process.

Let's turn to the seven-step approach to problem-solving. Here are the seven steps.

The Seven-Step Process

1. Define the problem.
2. Gather information.
3. Identify possible causes of the current problem.
4. Develop possible solutions.
5. Evaluate the solutions.
6. Implement the chosen solution.
7. Monitor and review.

1. **Define the problem.** You have to know what the problem is. Clarify the gap between the current situation and the desired outcome.
2. **Gather information.** Collect relevant data, feedback, and insights.
3. **Identify possible causes of the current problem.** Brainstorm potential root causes and their context.
4. **Develop some possible solutions** in light of the information you've uncovered. You may come up with several different ones. Encourage creativity while considering feasibility.
5. **Evaluate** all of the possible solutions, weigh the pros and cons, and be aware of biases before making a final decision.
6. **Implement the solution.** Assign tasks, set timelines, and deploy resources.
7. **Monitor and review.** Measure results, reflect on effectiveness, and tweak, fine-tune, and refine as needed.

A Case Study

Let's look at a case study of a fictitious company called Tech Solve Incorporated. This midsize software company has been facing a steady decline in sales for one of their core products. Upon initial review, the leadership suspected that there were multiple factors at play, such as increased competition and outdated marketing strategies.

Rather than jumping into quick fixes, the team decided to use the SWOT analysis and the seven-step approach to systematically uncover the root causes and craft an effective long-term solution.

They clarified that the primary issue was a 15 percent drop in quarterly sales for their flagship product. They gathered information, looking at sales reports, market research, and customer feedback so they could figure out what was happening.

Using that information, they identified the possible causes. They had a brainstorming session and conducted another SWOT analysis to break down the information that they collected into strengths, weaknesses, opportunities, and threats.

Then they moved on to developing possible solutions. Taking their insights from the SWOT, they proposed solutions that ranged from a product redesign to a reinvigorated marketing campaign. They also looked at potential partnerships to enhance product integration.

Once the company had all of these solutions in place, they weighed the pros and cons: they evaluated cost, time to market, and competitive positioning, and they decided to prioritize a partial product revamp and a targeted digital marketing push.

They implemented their solution, including the marketing campaign, which focused on new features and essential discounts for early adopters. They monitored their results for two quarters. When they reviewed, they saw a 12 percent uptick in sales and regained traction with their existing customers.

That's an illustration in a nutshell of the process of integrating SWOT with the seven-step process for making and implementing decisions.

Three Obstacles

Let's discuss how to turn strategic problem-solving principles into everyday practice, even in the face of real-world constraints. We're also going to talk about some common stumbling blocks, such as second-guessing, group resistance, and the analysis paralysis mentioned before.

1. **Second-guessing decisions.** When you second-guess decisions, you're overthinking or doubting your decisions after they have been made. This can erode confidence, make you look wishy-washy, and stall progress. This happens because you're afraid of failing or getting it wrong. Facing high stakes or a lack of clarity on success metrics or the next step can add to uncertainty and cause second-guessing. But what do you do?

    Trust the process. Lean on the strategic frameworks that you've established. If you've done your due diligence, you've collected your data, you've weighed pros and cons, and you recognize that constant second-guessing won't improve the outcome, you're going to be on the right track.

> **Three Common Obstacles**
> 1. Second-guessing decisions
> 2. Being stifled by the opinions of others
> 3. Analysis paralysis

Periodically check the result against your success and see if the data is supporting your decision. Can you move forward? If it looks like you cannot, go back and rethink it. Check and see where the breakdown might be instead of dwelling on the initial decision. Move forward to fix the problem.

2. **Being stifled by the opinions of others.** This can be a big challenge. Some on your team may feel overshadowed by a stronger personality, colleagues, or a group majority. Maybe important ideas have been lost or suppressed, leading to suboptimal solutions.

   This can happen because organizational hierarchies or existing power dynamics are in some form of struggle. There could also be conflict avoidance or fear of dissent in the company culture. Maybe you or someone else don't feel psychologically safe enough to come out with a differing opinion.

   Here you want to practice active communication skills and encourage clear, respectful dialogue. Paraphrase others' points to show that you understand before offering your own point of view. If you're in a leadership role, you want to be collaborative. Set the tone by inviting quieter team members to share. Actively solicit diverse opinions

with open-ended questions, not just ones that require yes or no answers. Establish meeting rules so that everyone gets a chance to speak. For sensitive topics, you could even consider anonymous feedback tools or voting systems.
3. **Analysis paralysis.** The challenge here is getting bogged down in endless data collection or debate. Sometimes we can debate ourselves into paralysis, stalling decision teams instead of enabling them to move forward and act.

    This will sometimes happen because of data leading to different conclusions. You have to look at the evidence and decide what it means, and you can become afraid of making the wrong choice. Differing opinions can also cause analysis paralysis in a team. As the old saying goes, a confused mind does nothing.

    To deal with this issue, set clear decision criteria. Define which data are critical versus merely nice to have. Once core criteria are met, move forward. Assign a strict time frame for research and deliberation. At deadline's end, commit to a decision. Test initially in smaller increments or pilot projects. If something isn't right, you can pivot quickly without losing large investments.

Driving Strategic Thinking

Now we want to talk about driving strategic thinking in a team. As already mentioned, ask open-ended questions: *what if, why can't we . . . ?* or *what would happen if . . . ?*

Mix up your team. Sometimes swapping out a couple of team members for others with fresh perspectives is just what you need to open up problem-solving dynamics.

Use brainstorming techniques. One kind is round-robin brainstorming. Here each person contributes one idea per turn, ensuring all voices are heard.

Then there is the SCAMPER method, which stands for *substituting, combining, adapting, modifying, putting to other uses, eliminating,* and *rearranging*. Although we won't go into it in detail here, you may want to research it as another brainstorming approach.

You want to encourage team members to challenge the status quo. Praise team members who suggest unconventional ideas, even if they're not viable. Acknowledge these members for sharing their thoughts. Don't make them feel, "I shouldn't have said that; I shouldn't have opened my mouth." That will only defeat your purpose.

Reward, experiment, acknowledge, and share learning from failed trials. Again, a failure is just another opportunity to learn.

It's also valuable to maintain a reflective culture. Hold postmortem discussions to go back and dissect what worked and what didn't. Debrief the project, debrief the decision, and decide what you can learn for the next time.

An Action Plan

Now that we've gone through all of this information, it's time to put together an action plan to get into strategic thinking and decision-making processes.

Begin by identifying one to three specific goals. These could be something as simple as completing a SWOT analysis for an upcoming project or implementing a two-week pilot test of a new idea.

Apply the SMART goals formula. To repeat, SMART stands for *specific, measurable, achievable, relevant,* and *time-bound*—all of which should apply to your goals.

Build accountability. Share goals with the team, and encourage participants to inform a colleague, manager, or mentor about their new commitment. Sharing fosters support, keeps you on track, and ensures that goals don't quietly blip off the radar.

Set a timeline. Specify check-in intervals, whether weekly or monthly, to evaluate progress, discuss hurdles, and celebrate small wins.

Look at the long-term vision to maintain momentum. Reassess your goals every thirty to ninety days, adjust them based on outcome and evolving priorities, and continue to integrate strategic problem-solving habits into your ongoing project.

Overcoming obstacles like second-guessing and external pressures in order to make problem-solving a consistent practice is not always easy, but it is highly productive. If you persevere, the result will be an environment where challenges are tackled proactively, innovation thrives, and each individual is empowered to drive forward-thinking strategic solutions.

Key Points in This Chapter

The chapter has been intended to help you improve your analytical ability, guide critical thinking, and provide practical and effective strategies for solving problems and making decisions that have lasting outcomes.

We began with the subject of making a decision versus strategically solving a problem. We proceeded to the six habits of strategic thinkers and to recognizing your thinking and problem-solving style. We went on to cover tools for strategic problem-solving, such as the SWOT analysis and the seven-step approach. Finally, we discussed applying this material and overcoming common obstacles.

EIGHT

Developing a Growth Mindset

This chapter will explore how a growth mindset can transform the way you approach challenges, adapt to change, and continually improve, both personally and professionally.

A growth mindset is the belief that you can develop your abilities and intelligence with effort, learning, and persistence. It's about seeing challenges as opportunities and seeing failures as stepping stones to growth. In today's fast-paced and ever-changing world, this mindset isn't just nice to have: it is essential, whether you're navigating career changes, tackling personal goals, or leading a team through uncertain times. Developing a growth mindset can unlock your potential and help you thrive.

In this chapter, we'll cover how to identify and evaluate your current mindset, the factors that shape how we think and grow, and practical strategies for letting go of negativity and building resilience. We'll examine tools for navigating challenges, embracing change, and building resilience. We'll identify opportunities for growth and show how to create a plan for continual improvement.

Throughout this chapter, you'll find suggestions for self-guided exercises and activities. These are designed to help you apply what you learn.

Before we begin, take a moment to reflect on where you are now and what area of your life or work you want to improve. As you move through each section, think about how you can apply these insights to your own journey.

Fixed versus Growth Mindsets

To develop a growth mindset, it's important to recognize where you stand today. Psychologist Carol S. Dweck, who pioneered the concept of the growth mindset, defines it as the belief that abilities can be developed through dedication and hard work. In contrast, a fixed mindset is the belief that abilities are static: you're either good at something or you're not. If you've ever thought, "I'm just not good at math," or "I'm a natural at public speaking," you've experienced the influence of the fixed mindset.

Someone with a fixed mindset tends to avoid challenges. Someone with a growth mindset may not love the challenges but will embrace them as opportunities to grow. A fixed-mindset person will give up easily when faced with obstacles and setbacks, whereas a growth-mindset person perseveres. The fixed mindset views effort as fruitless or unnecessary, whereas a growth mindset views it as a path to mastery. The fixed mindset tends to ignore constructive feedback. The growth mindset welcomes feedback in order to improve. The

The Fixed Mindset

- Avoids challenges.
- Gives up easily.
- Views effort as fruitless or unnecessary.
- Ignores constructive feedback.
- Feels threatened by others' success.
- Believes that abilities and intelligence are static.
- Prefers to stick to what they already know.
- Focuses on proving themselves.

The Growth Mindset

- Embraces challenges as opportunities to grow.
- Perseveres.
- Views effort as a path to mastery.
- Welcomes feedback in order to improve.
- Finds inspiration in others' success.
- Believes that abilities and intelligence can be developed over time.
- Thrives on learning and adapting.
- Focuses on improving themselves instead of proving themselves.

fixed mindset will feel threatened by others' success, whereas a growth mindset will find inspiration in it.

The fixed mindset believes that both abilities and intelligence are static, whereas a growth mindset person believes that they can be developed over time. A fixed-mindset person prefers to stick to what they already know, whereas one with a growth mindset thrives on learning and adapting to new things. A fixed-mindset person focuses on proving themselves instead of improving. A growth-mindset person focuses on growth and learning—improving themselves instead of proving themselves.

Take another glance at these characteristics. Think about yourself: which side do you lean toward? You may find that in some circumstances, you have more of the traits of someone with a fixed mindset, whereas in other circumstances you might demonstrate more of a growth mindset.

When faced with a challenge, a fixed mindset might say, "I can't do this. I'm not smart enough." A growth mindset would say, "This is hard, but I can learn how to do it." This is a subtle but powerful shift that changes your approach to obstacles and opportunities.

Think about a recent challenge or setback that you faced. How did you respond? Did you shy away, or did you view it as a chance to grow?

Here's a self-assessment exercise that you can try: Write down three challenges that you have faced. For each, note your initial reaction. Then ask yourself, was it more aligned with a growth mindset or a fixed mindset? Having a fixed mindset in some or many areas doesn't mean that you're stuck. Awareness is the first step to change.

Once you've identified your current mindset, you can start to reframe it. Instead of thinking, "I can't do this," try adding the word *yet*: "I can't do this *yet*." That small shift opens the door to possibilities and reminds you that growth is a process.

Your mindset is not fixed. It can change, and that starts with your awareness. Take some time to do a self-assessment and reflect on your findings: this small step can have a big impact.

Factors That Shape Your Mindset

Now that you've identified where you stand, let's dive into the factors that shape your mindset. Understanding these influences is key to unlocking long-term growth. A mindset doesn't form in isolation. It's shaped by a combination of upbringing, experiences, and environment. Let's explore these factors in more detail.

One of the most significant influences on mindset is upbringing. Messages we receive as children, like, "You are so smart" or "You'll never be good at math," can plant the seeds of a mindset. If you've ever been praised solely for your natural talent, you might have developed a fixed mindset. In that case, you might fear failure, because it could prove that you're not as talented as people think you are. On the other hand, being praised for your effort encourages the belief that you can develop skills and intelligence over time.

Here's a specific example of these two approaches and what they might sound like: (1) "Wow! You are an amazing artist. I love that drawing." (2) "I can see that you've worked hard to create a beautiful drawing." Which statement promotes a fixed mindset, and which promotes a growth mindset? As we've seen, a fixed mindset arises from being praised solely for natural talent, so the first statement promotes more

> **Factors That Shape Mindset**
> - Upbringing
> - Experiences
> - Environment
> - Internal dialogue

of a fixed mindset. The second statement promotes a growth mindset, because you are being praised for your effort.

Armed with this awareness, you can now influence a growth mindset in your children, your team, and your peers, and you can even use it to influence a growth mindset for yourself.

Think back to your childhood. What messages shaped your beliefs about your abilities? A father may tell his child, "You'll never amount to anything. You'll never graduate high school." He may not intend to scar the child for life; these messages may have been meant to motivate the child. Nevertheless, such messages affect one's beliefs about oneself. It may take decades to overcome some of these limiting beliefs.

Think back to your childhood. What messages shaped your beliefs about your abilities?

What is one experience from your life that aligns with this factor? How has it influenced your mindset?

Another powerful factor is how you've handled challenges and setbacks in the past. Experiences like failing at a project, receiving critical feedback, or navigating significant life challenges can either reinforce a fixed mindset or cultivate a growth mindset, depending on how you interpret those experiences.

Here's a tip: the next time you face a challenge, ask yourself, "What can I learn from this experience?" Even difficult situations can be valuable teachers.

Again, think back to your childhood. What life experiences and challenges have shaped your beliefs about your abilities? What is one experience that stands out from your life that aligns with this factor? How has it influenced your mindset?

You can also apply this tip to other parts of your past. Ask yourself, "What can I learn from this past experience?"

Environment plays a crucial role too. The people around you—family, friends, colleagues, bosses—can either encourage growth or hold you back. Being surrounded by supportive, growth-oriented individuals can inspire you to take risks and embrace learning. Conversely, a critical or overly competitive environment may foster self-doubt and limit growth. Take stock of your environment. Are you surrounded by people and situations that encourage growth?

What one person or situation is affecting you in this way? How has it influenced your mindset? If it is promoting a fixed mindset, what small changes can you make to foster a more supportive atmosphere? This doesn't mean that you must end a relationship with a friend or a coworker, but you might consider establishing a few boundaries or spending less time with that person.

An example: a woman named Kathy was going through some personal struggles. She had a friend, Sheila, who was a great support to her during that time. Sheila listened and empathized with Kathy to the point of pity.

Kathy started to notice a trend with Sheila: When she had a struggle that was resolved, she would immediately find something else wrong in her life. If Kathy suggested a way to solve it, Sheila would get angry with her.

Kathy finally realized that Sheila liked being a victim of life's circumstances. The situation didn't matter: it could have been a work problem or a problem with a relationship or even a family member. On the one hand, Sheila was a great support to Kathy when she was in a bad place. On the other hand, when Kathy actually wanted to move on and beyond, Sheila wanted her to stay in a negative place. Eventually, Kathy started spending less and less time with Sheila and started feeling better and more positive. This was not a coincidence.

Consider a person or a situation in your life. What small changes can you make to foster a more supportive atmosphere?

Finally, our internal dialogue shapes how we see ourselves and the world. Fixed mindset thinking often sounds like, "I can't do this" or "I'm just not good enough." Growth mindset reframes those thoughts into, "I can't do this *yet*, but I can learn."

Here's a beginner's self-awareness activity: Over the next week, pay attention to your self-talk. For every negative or limiting thought, try to reframe it into a positive, growth-oriented statement.

Pay attention to your self-talk.

Self-talk often follows the words "I am . . ." Here's a simple way to reframe "I am" statements. Write down two or three negative "I am" statements that you regularly find yourself saying about yourself. Examples are "I am ugly" and "I am weak."

Flip the statements. What is the opposite of that negative statement to you personally? You may decide that the opposite of "I am weak" is, "I am strong," and the opposite of "I am ugly" is "I am beautiful."

All of the words in the new statement must be positive: no double negatives. "I am not weak" doesn't work, because you're still using the word "weak" to describe yourself. Think of it this way: when someone says, don't look left, what do you normally do? Usually you look left. It's the same way with double negatives. Statements like "I am not weak," "I am not ugly," and "I am not stupid" are no better than saying that you are weak, ugly, and stupid.

Come up with two or three positive "I am" statements. Implement a practice of saying your new "I am" statements daily. The best time of day for affirmations is in the morning. Even if you accumulate a dozen or more positive "I am" statements, it will only take a couple of minutes in the morning to say them.

The best application of this practice is to say these positive statements in the mirror while looking at yourself. It's not necessary to say them out loud. You can, for example, say them to yourself while using an electric toothbrush timed for two minutes. Find the best place for you to say your "I am" statements every morning. Once you master this practice, flipping statements like, "I'm not smart enough" or "I'm not good enough" will become easy.

>>>

Negative factors may have shaped your mindset, but they don't define it.

>>>

Here's the takeaway. While these negative factors may have shaped your mindset, they don't define it. By becoming aware of their influence, you can take control and shift your perspective.

Cultivating Positivily

Now that we understand the factors shaping our mindset, let's talk about a critical step in developing a growth mindset: letting go of negativity and cultivating positivity. Negativity can weigh us down and make it harder to see opportunities and embrace growth. The good news is that you can actively shift your perspective and build habits that foster positivity.

>>>

You can build habits that foster positivity.

>>>

Let's start by identifying common sources of negativity. These might include self-doubt, which may include thoughts like, "I'm not good enough." That's an example of self-doubt: comparison, measuring yourself against others' achievements. You'll never win the comparison game. It's an endless game that always results in a feeling of negativity. There is also fear of failure: avoiding risks because you're afraid of making mistakes. Finally there is external criticism, negative feedback, or judgment from others.

Recognizing these sources of negativity is the first step to addressing them. Once you are aware, you can take action.

Here are a few simple strategies you can start using today. The first one is the "three positive" exercises. At the end of each day, write down three positive things that happened that day. They do not have to be big events: small, simple wins count. For example, "I finished a task on time"; "I enjoyed a great conversation with a friend"; "I watched an on-demand course." All of these could be small wins, but remember to find three.

Reframe negative thoughts. When you catch yourself thinking negatively, pause and ask, is this thought helpful? Then try to reframe it. For example, instead of thinking, "I failed at this," say, "I learned something valuable from this experience."

When you start your positive "I am" statement practice, you may notice negative thoughts that you have about yourself throughout the day. One remedy is the technique of saying either "cancel" or "delete" when you find yourself doing this. Then replace the negative thought or statement with a positive one. In sum, you catch yourself, you say "cancel" or "delete," and then restate the thought in a positive way.

The last is gratitude practice. Spend a few minutes each morning reflecting on things you're grateful for. Gratitude shifts your focus from what's lacking to what's abundant in your life. You may want to start by writing down three things you are grateful for each day.

You can also be grateful for what you're creating in your life, although you may not have actually achieved it yet. The idea is to be grateful for what is to come. Here's an example of a gratitude statement for something you're creating: "I am grateful for the opportunity to demonstrate my value to the team I work with."

Letting go of negativity is only half of the equation. To truly adopt a growth mindset, you need to actively cultivate positivity, As we've already suggested, you can surround yourself with positive influences and spend time with people who inspire and uplift you. If your circle includes individuals who are often negative, consider setting boundaries to protect your mindset. You might seek out a new group to join. Consider taking a class at the community college or volunteer to serve those less fortunate than you. One woman, a lawyer with a lot of stress, joined a pizza meetup group. Something that simple can change your perspective and put you around positive influences.

Set intentional goals. Having clear, meaningful goals gives you something positive to work towards. Break these goals into manageable steps and celebrate your progress along the way.

Finally, engage in activities that spark joy, such as a hobby, exercising, or spending time in nature. Prioritize activities that make you feel good and recharge your energy.

Here's a simple exercise you can try: Write down one limiting belief you have about yourself, like, "I'm not good at public speaking." Next, rewrite it as a positive affirmation such as, "I am learning to become a confident speaker." Repeat this affirmation daily for the next two to three weeks and notice how it begins to shift your perspective.

This is not necessarily a quick fix: it does require commitment to daily practice. You'll be able to change some of your beliefs in a week or two, but you have to have the patience and dedication to rewrite deep-seated beliefs and truly believe them.

Deep-seated beliefs take time to rewrite, and more importantly, they take time to believe. One woman said, "I am beautiful" every morning in the bathroom mirror. After about three years of daily practice, she finally believed it. It took three years to erase a belief that she had had for thirty years. This was not a big price to pay.

Negativity is not permanent.

The most important point is this: negativity is not permanent. You can let go of what's holding you back with intentional effort, and you can replace it with habits and thoughts that propel you forward. As you let go of negativity and cultivate positivity, you create the foundation for resilience and adaptability. These qualities are essential for navigating the inevitable changes and challenges that we all face. Change is one of life's constants, whether it's a shift in your career, your personal life, or your daily routines.

> Resilience and adaptability form the foundation of a growth mindset.

Resilience and Adaptability

Resilience and adaptability go hand in hand. Resilience gives you the strength to face challenges, while adaptability allows you to embrace and thrive through change. You can think of resilience as bouncing back and adapting as bouncing forward. Together, they form the foundation of a growth mindset.

The pandemic of the early 2020s is a perfect example of the importance of resilience and adaptability. At the beginning, everyone was saying, "Let's wait it out." Three weeks became three months, and three months became three years.

In 2021, Fry's Electronics closed their doors because of changing consumer shopping habits and challenges posed by the pandemic. They did not have an online option for shopping. In the third quarter of 2020, another electronics chain, Best Buy, had their best quarter in twenty-five years. Nine months later, Fry's closed their doors for good. Could this have been due to Fry's failure to adapt to the pandemic—a time where the public learned how to shop online?

When faced with change, people often react in one of two ways: resistance, possibly stemming from fear or uncertainty, or adaptation: seeing change as an opportunity to grow. Why does change feel so challenging?

It's natural to fear the unknown and cling to familiar routines. Change often triggers the brain's threat response, making us feel uncomfortable or even resistant. Resilience helps us manage these feelings. Here's the good news: you can retrain your brain to view change as a positive force, one that leads to growth and new opportunities.

Thriving through Change

Here are six strategies to help you not just survive but thrive through change.

1. **Focus on what you can control.** When change feels overwhelming, pause and ask yourself, what's within my control? Focusing on actionable steps like organizing your tasks or seeking advice can reduce stress and create a sense of empowerment.
2. **Reframe change as an opportunity.** Instead of saying, "Why is this happening to me?" ask, "What can I learn from this?" This shift of perspective helps you see challenges as stepping stones to growth rather than roadblocks.
3. **Take small, consistent steps.** Adapting to change doesn't have to happen overnight. Break down the process into

> **Six Steps for Thriving through Change**
> 1. Focus on what you can control.
> 2. Reframe change as an opportunity.
> 3. Take small, consistent steps.
> 4. Embrace failure as a learning opportunity.
> 5. Develop a support network.
> 6. Prioritize self-care.

manageable steps and celebrate each milestone. If you are transitioning to a new role, focus on learning just one new skill at a time.

4. **Embrace failure as a learning opportunity.** Failure isn't the opposite of success: it's part of the journey to success. When something doesn't go as planned, ask yourself, "What did I learn from this experience?" Write down your insights and consider how you can apply them moving forward.
5. **Develop a support network.** Resilience is not a solo act. Surround yourself with people who uplift and support you, whether it's friends, family, or colleagues. A strong support system can make all the difference.
6. **Prioritize self-care.** Taking care of your physical, mental and emotional health will lay the foundation for resilience. Simple practices like getting enough sleep, eating well, and setting aside time for relaxation can boost your ability to handle stress.

Reflecting on Recent Changes

Here's a self-guided activity to help you navigate change: Reflect on a recent change you've experienced. How did you respond to it? What strengths or strategies did you use? Now think about one action you can take to enhance your resilience and adaptability for similar situations in the future. By recognizing your past successes, you can build confidence in your ability to handle whatever comes next.

Write down one change you're currently experiencing or anticipating. Reflect on the challenges it presented or is presenting. Acknowledge the change in how it makes you feel—excited, anxious, or uncertain. Make a note of those feelings and then outline what you did or can do. Note how you responded, or can respond, with resilience or adaptability. Then set a positive intention, such as, "I will approach similar changes with curiosity and openness." Creating a change response plan can transform uncertainty into clarity and action.

Let's consider an example: You've just been assigned a new project at work, one that feels outside your comfort zone. To make it even more challenging, you recently faced disappointment because you did not get a promotion you applied for. Instead of letting these situations hold you back, you can adapt by learning. Dive into the project with curiosity and a willingness to develop new skills. Build resilience by reflecting. Consider what feedback or lessons you can take from the missed promotion. Use this insight to strengthen your contributions to the new project. Reframe challenges as opportunities. View both situations as stepping stones to future success and not setbacks.

Resilience isn't just an individual trait; it's also essential for teams. As a leader, you can help your team build resilience by encouraging open communication and a supportive environment, recognizing and celebrating small wins to boost morale and leading by example. Show your team how to navigate challenges with a growth mindset.

You don't have to be a supervisor or manager to be a leader; you can still lead by applying these concepts. But if you are a boss, it is essential that you make failure and learning and growth safe in your team's environment. You do that by sharing your own failures, setbacks, and roadblocks and how you overcame them. That will make it safe for everyone on the team to do the same.

> Change is not something to fear.
> It's an opportunity to grow.

Change is not something to fear. It's an opportunity to grow. You can thrive through any transition by focusing on what you can control, reframing challenges, taking consistent steps forward, embracing failure as an opportunity, building yourself a support network, and practicing self-care.

The Example of Netflix

Netflix offers a powerful example of resilience and adaptability during a major market shift. In the early 2000s, the company faced declining interest in DVD rentals as streaming technology began to emerge. Recognizing the change, Netflix shifted its focus from its DVD-by-mail service to embrace streaming content.

Here's some of their key actions: First, they anticipated change. Netflix identified early on that the future of entertainment was in digital streaming, not physical media. This foresight allowed the company to start investing in streaming infrastructures before many of its competitors, and then adapting the business strategy. Despite initial backlash from customers and significant operational challenges, Netflix transitioned to a subscription-based streaming model. This required not only technological changes but reshaping its brand and operations.

Netflix increased their resilience by producing their own content. This move helped the company differentiate itself in an increasingly competitive streaming landscape, and they learned from missteps. Netflix also demonstrated resilience by learning from mistakes such as the poorly received attempt to separate its DVD and streaming businesses into two brands. The company acknowledged the misstep, reversed course, and refocused its efforts.

What was the outcome? Netflix is now one of the most recognized and successful streaming platforms globally, with over 302 million subscribers as of late 2024. Its ability to adapt to change and maintain resilience during difficult times has ensured its survival and growth in a rapidly evolving industry.

In the next section, we'll talk about identifying actionable growth strategies and creating a plan for continual improvement.

Growth Opportunities

We've explored how to understand your mindset, navigate challenges, build resilience, and be adaptable. Now let's focus on identifying actionable growth opportunities. This step is all about turning your insights into tangible, practical steps for personal and professional development.

Growth opportunities are moments when you can learn, improve, and stretch beyond your comfort zone. They might not always be obvious, but with the right mindset, you can train yourself to spot them in everyday situations. Think of growth opportunities as seeds. You plant them with effort, nurture them with consistency, and watch them grow into meaningful progress.

Here's how to start identifying areas for growth:

1. **Assess your current skills and goals.** Reflect on your strengths and your areas for improvement. Ask yourself, what skills or knowledge do I need to reach my next goal?
2. **Look for challenges.** Challenges often disguise themselves as growth opportunities, whether it's taking on a new project, learning a difficult skill, or stepping into a leadership role. These experiences push you to grow.
3. **Seek feedback.** Sometimes growth opportunities come from an outside perspective. Ask a mentor, a colleague, a friend, "What's one area where you think I could grow?" You could even ask this of your team if you're a manager. They would love to give their feedback and will be pleased by your trusting them with that question. Feedback can provide valuable insights that you might not see on your own.

> **Identifying Growth Areas**
> 1. Assess your current skills and goals.
> 2. Look for challenges.
> 3. Seek feedback.

Once you've identified your growth opportunities, it's time to take action. Here are some tools to help you get started. First, set **SMART** goals. As we've already seen, the **S** stands for *specific*. Define exactly what you want to achieve. **M** is for *measurable*. Decide how you'll track the progress. **A** is for *achievable*. Make sure your goal is realistic, but maybe with a little bit of a stretch or a reach to achieve that goal.

R: make your goals *relevant*. Align them with your larger goals. Align them with your own personal mission and vision for your work, your career, your business, and your life. Consider the mission and vision of your organization, your department, and your boss. Making your goals relevant increases the *why* behind them, increasing your chances for success.

The **T** stands for *time-bound*. To stay accountable, set a deadline. Instead of saying, "I want to improve my communication skills," you could say, "I will complete a public speaking course and deliver three presentations by the end of the quarter."

After setting SMART goals, create a growth plan. Those of you with access to Pryor on-demand resources can find valuable additional resources. Search the words "growth plan" and check out the available resources, including one called "an action plan for growth." Its objective is to outline your goals, determine the steps to achieve them, and establish checkpoints to review your progress.

Also build growth habits. Incorporate both daily and weekly habits that align with your goals. If you want to improve your time management, commit to planning your day every morning and planning your week at least once a week on Saturday or Sunday. Plan out the week, and then each day, you check on the plan for the day.

Take fifteen minutes to create your growth plan. Write down one skill or area that you'd like to improve. Identify one action step that you can take immediately, and then set a timeline for achieving your first milestone. Progress is a process. Every small step adds up over time, so take the time to notice your progress.

Let's look at an example of a growth action plan: Imagine that you want to become a better leader. Your growth plan might look like this:

The goal: to develop stronger communication skills with your team. The action steps: to enroll in a leadership communication workshop. Schedule one-on-one check-ins with your team members at least once a month. Practice active listening during meetings. To set a timeline, determine to implement all steps within the next three months.

Growth opportunities are all around you. By setting clear goals, taking consistent action, and staying committed to your plan, you can unlock your potential and create meaningful progress in your personal and your professional life.

Consider one goal you have for yourself. Recall the question from the beginning of this chapter: what area of your life or work do you want to improve? Is your original answer still valid? Are there other areas that you want to improve? What one area of your life or your work will you commit to improving?

Next Steps

Here are some next steps you can take to continue building your growth mindset.

- Complete your growth plan. Use the steps given to outline your goals and action steps.
- Revisit the exercises.
- Incorporate practices like gratitude, journaling, and self-reflection into your routine.
- Share what you've learned with others. Teaching others is a great way to reinforce your own learning. Share these concepts with a friend, colleague, mentor, or your team.

Then, who knows? Maybe you can establish some accountability partners to apply what you have learned and shared and to explore additional resources. Check out Carol S. Dweck's book *Mindset* and her TED Talk, where she talks about using the word *yet* or *not yet*. Consider additional courses and on-demand resources to deepen your learning. Remember, growth is a journey, not a destination. Take it one step at a time, and trust in your ability to learn, grow, and adapt.

Key Points in This Chapter

In this chapter, we started by exploring how to understand your current mindset and recognize whether it's a fixed or a growth mindset. You may have found that you have both a fixed mindset and a growth mindset in different areas. Then we looked at the factors that shape your mindset: your upbringing, experiences, environment, and self-talk. We suggested that you reflect on some of the major influences that have formed your mindset. We moved on to practical strategies for letting go of negativity and cultivating positivity, including simple exercises like the three positives practice and reframing your thoughts.

Next, we discussed how to thrive through change by focusing on what you can control, reframing challenges as opportunities, and taking small consistent steps forward. We also explored how to build resilience by embracing failure, developing a support network, and prioritizing self-care. Finally, we looked into how to identify actionable growth opportunities, set smart goals, and create a growth plan.

The power of a growth mindset lies not just in what you learn but in what you do. Please revisit these exercises and activities and apply them daily.

Your growth journey can start here. Keep challenging yourself, embrace new opportunities, and celebrate every step of progress along the way.

AFTERWORD

It is, perhaps, difficult to summarize the many lessons conveyed in the preceding chapters. Even so, certain key elements stand out.

The first is confidence. While some people naturally have more confidence than others, it is not a static quality. It can be enhanced by the methods we have explored, such as eliminating negative self-talk; viewing mistakes and failures as learning opportunities; and developing a personal style whereby your appearance, manners, posture, and tone of voice inspire trust and confidence at first sight.

Another major theme is effective communication, without which true leadership is impossible. We explored how to develop an assertive communication style, which conveys respect both for yourself and for those you are addressing. We have also discussed the crucial element of clarity of thought and expression.

A third theme was team building, which requires, above all else, clear insight into the people you are working with and how their differences in character and style will affect—and can enhance—the team's performance as a whole. We saw how the best management style steers a middle course between passivity and people-pleasing on the one hand and arrogance and confrontation on the other.

If we were to boil down the essence of this book into one central element, perhaps it would be personal decency. Managers who excel and advance convey honesty, sincerity, and genuine care for those they manage. Dedication to the tasks at hand—however important—can never completely override the fact that managers work with people and can never lead them effectively without respectful and genuine consideration of them as individuals.

www.ingramcontent.com/pod-product-compliance
Lightning Source LLC
LaVergne TN
LVHW021700060526
838200LV00050B/2444